# More Praise for *Dynamic Strategy-Making*

"The authors' view of strategy-making is highly relevant to the fast pace of the 21st century. Their insights make this book essential for leaders who seek to be involved in charting the long-term direction of their organizations!"

—Jay W. Lorsch, Louis E. Kirstein Professor of Human Relations, Harvard Business School; and author, *Back to the Drawing Board* and *Aligning the Stars*

"The authors make a convincing case that strategy is too important to leave to the strategists. They provide a fresh perspective on the domain of strategic management as a comprehensive organizational process of learning and development, reframing our traditional lenses and inviting much needed cross functional discourse on the very essence of sustaining competitiveness."

—Dr. Roland Deiser, chairman, European Corporate Learning Forum; and former dean, DaimlerChrysler Corporate University

# Dynamic Strategy-Making

## A Real-Time Approach for the 21st Century Leader

Larry E. Greiner
and Thomas G. Cummings

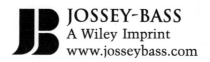
JOSSEY-BASS
A Wiley Imprint
www.josseybass.com

Published by Jossey-Bass
A Wiley Imprint
989 Market Street, San Francisco, CA 94103-1741—www.josseybass.com

Jossey-Bass books and products are available through most bookstores. To contact Jossey-Bass directly call our Customer Care Department within the U.S. at 800-956-7739, outside the U.S. at 317-572-3986, or fax 317-572-4002.

Jossey-Bass also publishes its books in a variety of electronic formats. Some content that appears in print may not be available in electronic books.

**Library of Congress Cataloging-in-Publication Data**

Greiner, Larry E.
Dynamic strategy-making: a real-time approach for the 21st century leader / Larry E. Greiner and Thomas G. Cummings.
    p. cm.
Includes bibliographical references and index.
ISBN 978-0-7879-9663-5 (cloth)
1. Strategic planning. 2. Leadership. I. Cummings, Thomas G. II. Title.
HD30.28.G739 2009
658.4'012—dc22

2008055672

Printed in the United States of America

FIRST EDITION

*HB Printing*          10 9 8 7 6 5 4 3 2 1

# Contents

# Preface

Recent business maelstroms have not been reassuring to managers concerned with strategic planning. On the radar screens of CEOs, the high price of oil, global warming, the financial credit crisis, and terrorism ripple through the usual turbulence of global competition, technological innovation, and hostile takeovers. What will tomorrow bring? In this world of constant, uncertain surprise, many companies are on the decline or are being swallowed up by stronger ones. The outlook has been poor for many organizations, and the fallout on the negative side has been huge.

In 1994, Henry Mintzberg, in his classic book, *The Rise and Fall of Strategic Planning*, astutely declared that the practice of strategic planning is an oxymoron: it has generally failed because it eliminates creative thinking. In our opinion, it has taken over a decade for CEOs and managers to accept Mintzberg's keen insight. Most organizations have continued to do strategic planning as a ritualistic annual exercise. However, the lethal heat and pace of real-world competition today spell an end to that neglect. Ours is now a world of global companies and hypercompetition, sparking real-time events that were not pervasive in 1994.

Bureaucratic thinking still casts a pall over the way many firms do strategic planning. Even if their organizations aren't bureaucratic, the planning process remains rigid and inflexible because it occurs only once a year, conducted solely by top management, highly formalized in its format and detail, and communicated impersonally down the chain of command. And frequently it is tied to the budget and capital spending cycle. Execution occurs in a similar way: responsibility for results is assigned to line managers, who send their version of the strategic plan down the chain of command. It is not even a strategy at this point but a set of assignments to subordinates. It rarely reaches the frontline workforce. No wonder that these plans are weak on implementation and that managers report on surveys how unhappy they are with this planning process (Dye and Sibony, 2007). All of this is hardly in keeping with being able to plan today.

Fast-moving events surrounding organizations have made formal annual approaches to strategic planning outdated. And they have thrown a challenge at consultants who are used to billing by time for studies and other methods that extend over several months.

This book is about a new real-time approach to strategy-making for leaders to take when faced with increasingly global, perpetual hypercompetition. It proposes a new concept, *dynamic strategy-making*, which takes on form as a sustainable and renewable strategic system permeating the organization, making it relevant to today's world. The system charts direction while remaining flexible and timely, possessing built-in capabilities for involvement and revision as new events dictate.

We believe our approach is unique and innovative. To help managers in designing a strategic system, it offers (1) the *4D framework* to make a strategic assessment and formulate strategic content, (2) *four key elements* to transfer their content conclusions to (3) a *statement of strategic direction* that is concrete, clear and actionable, (4) while using *guided involvement* as a process to stimulate strategic content and build commitment to a new direction, (5) all aided by the support of a new kind of consultant providing strategy facilitation.

This is not a book about strategy as an abstract property of organizations; it is an attempt to close the theory-practice gap. It is a how-to book founded on existing theory and research. It avoids academic jargon, opting for action-focused steps to take. The strategy field, long dominated by academics and consultants, is in need of simplified, concrete approaches that leaders can use in a do-it-yourself mode. And interestingly, at least one traditional, somewhat tired, term, *strategic management*, may be due for a dynamic update.

We are writing first and foremost for today's and tomorrow's leaders of organizations: for profit, not-for-profit, and public. These individuals are searching for a new approach to strategy-making because their formal planning methods no longer work. But you need not be a CEO to find useful knowledge in this book. It is relevant to a number of other audiences: aspiring students in business schools who want to become leaders, strategy consultants trying to improve how they work, and experienced managers looking to become senior leaders in their companies. Academics should find it interesting for its focus on the practical application of their theories and research in innovative ways.

Skeptics may think, "We have heard it all before," but we know it has not been said in this way in the same place and with the same practical guidelines. The concept of a real-time strategic system, including how to install and maintain it, is new. This isn't old-style strategic planning redressed or a new age vision-setting process that strains credibility. While we think *dynamic strategy-making* is advanced in its formulation, it is still at an early stage of development, and we hope that future scholars, consultants, and managers will refine and improve it with new approaches and methods.

# The Authors

Larry E. Greiner is professor of management and organization in the Marshall School of Business at the University of Southern California (USC). He received his M.B.A. and D.B.A. degrees from the Harvard Business School, where he has served on the faculty. He has also been on the faculty of INSEAD in France and other schools. He currently serves as founding academic director of USC's Global Executive M.B.A. Program in Shanghai, China. Previously he was academic director of USC's top-ranked Executive Program for fourteen years. He is former chairperson of the Management Department at USC, as well as chairperson of the Organization Development Division and the Managerial Consultation Divisions of the national Academy of Management.

Greiner is the author of numerous publications on the subjects of organization growth and development, management consulting, and strategic change. His most recent book, *The Contemporary Consultant* (with Flemming Poulfelt), has been widely recognized as a major contribution to the field. Among his many articles is the *Harvard Business Review* classic, "Evolution and Revolution as Organizations Grow." In 1999, he and Arvind Bhambri won the McKinsey Prize from the Strategic Management Society for their paper, "New CEOs and Strategic Change Across Industries." Greiner has served on numerous editorial and corporate boards and has consulted with many companies and government agencies.

Thomas G. Cummings is a leading international scholar and consultant on designing and implementing high-performance organizations. He is currently professor and chair of the Department of Management and Organization at the Marshall School of Business, University of Southern California. He is also a senior member of the Center for Effective Organizations at USC, a world leader in applied knowledge of high-involvement organizations, team-based work, innovative reward systems, and large-scale change. He received B.S. and M.B.A. degrees from Cornell University and a Ph.D. in business administration from the University of California at Los Angeles.

Cummings is widely recognized in both business and academic communities for his many contributions to knowledge about strategic change and high-performing organizations. He has authored over seventy articles and twenty-two books, including the critically acclaimed *Self-Designing Organizations: Learning How to Create High Performance* (with Susan Mohrman)   and *Organization Development and Change, Ninth Edition* (with Chris Worley).

Cummings was formerly president of the Western Academy of Management, chair of the Organization Development and Change Division of the Academy of Management, and founding editor of the *Journal of Management Inquiry*. He was the sixty-first president of the Academy of Management, the largest professional association of management scholars in the world, with a total membership of over eighteen thousand. He is listed in *American Men and Women of Science* and *Who's Who in America*.

# 1

# DEMISE OF STRATEGIC PLANNING AND ITS DYNAMIC REPLACEMENT

Today's organizations face a 24/7 world that is fast-paced, complex, and uncertain. Competition can be intense around the clock throughout the world. Competitive advantage can disappear overnight. Even the smallest companies can enter global markets easily, relying on Web-based transactions and unique products and services. New technologies can quickly make products and services obsolete. A hostile acquirer, using borrowed capital, can oust a firm's management and restructure its assets in a blink (Gladwell, 2005).

Unforeseen threats and political instability can swiftly render even the largest companies vulnerable and insecure; witness the recent financial crisis and energy problems. Some scholars say that companies in these chaotic and uncertain situations are "competing on the edge," using strategies to cope with "structured chaos" (Brown and Eisenhardt, 1998). In situations such as these, profits can fall precipitously under slow, old-style strategic planning, but they can rise under quick-acting strategy.

Despite these perils, the world offers enormous opportunities for new competitive advantage and growth. Firms can create new markets globally through constant product innovation and novel marketing practices such as Web-based advertising. Outsourcing can reduce costs and enable companies to focus on what they do best. Computers and mobile technologies can speed decisions and communication. They can help firms create strategic networks and value chains that transcend time, place, and organizational boundaries.

1

There's even gold among the ruins for companies that can make real-time decisions. In 2005, Southwest Airlines had the strategic foresight to look ahead at the inevitable rise in oil prices and acted quickly to purchase oil at twenty-six dollars a barrel to cover 85 percent of its 2005 fuel needs as well as hedges for lower-priced fuel over the next four years, ending in 2009 at thirty-five dollars a barrel for 25 percent of their needs. In 2005, Southwest reported a profit for the first six months of $235 million when it could have been a $116 million dollar loss had it not locked in the fuel costs.

In another example, Japanese auto companies Toyota and Honda innovated their way out ahead of U.S. auto companies with their hybrids. Now GM, once the biggest auto company in the world, has a market value of $7 billion, and Toyota is at $200 billion. GM continued for years to sell gas guzzlers to customers who never thought that the price of gas could soar to the heights it did in 2008. Long known for its traditional planning bureaucracy, GM ignored long-established trends suggesting that oil prices were going to increase. The Japanese companies caught on to this long-term trend with some early decisions to invest in hybrid technology. This example signals that slow-moving leaders should get their own house in order by doing real-time strategy-making.

To cope with this fast-paced environment, executives and administrators are searching for ways to make their organizations' strategies more dynamic and action oriented. They are shunning traditional planning methods and looking for new approaches to strategy-making.

## An Ongoing Strategy-Making Process

In this book, we present a process for *dynamic strategy-making*, which enables organizations to thrive in today's competitive environments. It provides them with the capability to strategize continuously and execute rapidly, thereby forging a strong link between strategy and execution as an ongoing flow rather than sequential and separate events. It involves managers and frontline workers in tapping their ideas to build both substance and commitment to a new strategy. In all, it embeds strategy-making and implementation into the fabric of the organization—its structures, processes, and culture—to comprise what we call a strategic system. *Dynamic strategy-making* addresses both the content (the what of strategy) and the process (the how and who) of strategy-making.

It treats strategic content and process as inseparable and shows how they can be integrated to create a strategy that is relevant and implementable. *Dynamic strategy-making* bridges the gap between the competitive demands facing organizations today and the methods normally used to respond to them. Fast-paced environments require rapid strategic responses. Yet conventional approaches for planning and executing strategy are highly formal, detailed, and time-consuming, and they create, often unintentionally, obstacles to fast thinking and action. They obscure the fact that in rapidly changing environments, to be systematically late is to be systematically wrong.

In this book, we describe the forces shaping competitive environments. Then we say more about why traditional approaches to strategy-making have become obsolete and ineffective. We also present some popular alternatives, which we call *pseudo strategy-making*, that are unlikely to produce a coherent and sustainable strategy. We conclude the chapter with a call for real-time strategy-making and an outline of the rest of the book.

## Today's Fast-Paced Environments

*High velocity, hypercompetitive,* and *blur* are terms that describe the ever changing environment of organizations (Davis and Meyer, 1998). They signify the competitive world's accelerating change, complexity, and uncertainty. Fast-paced environments present firms with unprecedented threats and opportunities for success and call for real-time strategies and actions. A number of major trends contribute to fast-paced environments:

- Globalized markets (now notably including China and India) provide tremendous growth opportunities, but they also intensify competition. Even small companies are affected by global competitors (Bartlett and Ghoshal, 1998).

- Hypercompetition comes from sellers that lower costs yet still provide quality and service through outsourcing, unbundling the value chain, and joint ventures. Providing higher-quality service at lower cost is no longer a contradiction, as the successes of Costco, IKEA, and Ryanair make clear (Andersen and Poulfelt, 2006).

- Customers are better able to decide when they want to do business with "anyone, any time, any place." They can, for example, make stock transactions over a cell phone on the freeway late at night, do ATM banking at their choosing, or sell and order products on the Web when they want (Davis, 1996). Rapid technological and scientific advances lead to new products and services. Breakthroughs in bioscience and nanotechnology are just around the corner. Energy-saving products will lead the green revolution (Bytheway, 2007).

- Analysts and investors frequently pressure public companies to perform better. Firms cannot let up in seeking continuous growth and performance. The question analysts ask is, "What can you do for me today?" (Obstfeld and Taylor, 2005).

- The threat of being acquired, even through a hostile takeover, is often present. Investment firms with large equity funds seek to acquire underperforming firms and restructure them to sell them later for substantial returns (Buono and Bowditch, 2003).

- Employees are spread across the world and come from different cultural backgrounds. Many are in virtual jobs without close supervision and connected only by the Internet and e-mail. Corporate loyalty, once the prevailing attitude, has declined (O'Toole and Lawler, 2007).

- Political uncertainty and the threat of security problems characterize the global challenge. Some markets breed terrorism, requiring great security. The cost for security is increasing for many firms (Hough, 2007).

- Boards of directors, sensitive to governance scrutiny and their responsibilities, no longer trust verbal commitments and press top executives for written strategic plans. Many countries are requiring greater transparency and oversight through regulation (Nadler, Behan, and Nadler, 2006).

These trends, and many others, collapse the time frame within which organizations must respond to issues in their environments.

## Traditional Strategic Planning Is Obsolete

These trends place extraordinary demands on companies to make and execute strategies rapidly. They make obsolete the calendar-driven, formal strategic planning that has long been at the core of strategy-making. Traditional planning, with its related analytical models, lengthy studies, and planning staffs, is aimed at reducing uncertainty and risk. It is highly methodical and based on the common belief that if organizations can somehow collect and analyze sufficient data, they can rationally find solutions on their way to a better future. Thus, some firms pay millions to consulting firms for definitive studies that identify a likely and less risky path to a successful future. Others rely on staff planners to produce detailed budgets and initiatives. And some have even appointed chief strategy officers to oversee the strategy-making process.

The fast-moving world makes the shortfalls of traditional strategic planning look even more rigid and obsolete—too slow, too formal, and lacking in commitment from management and the wider workforce—reinforcing the cliché of "analysis paralysis."

## Disenchantment with Former Approaches

Increasingly, organizations and executives are rejecting these traditional, formalistic approaches:

- *Calendar-driven plans.* This yearly exercise by managers to review and update their strategic plans is typically conducted only at a certain time each year. But this timing is too rigid for the continual adjustments that are required to adapt to opportunities and threats that can appear every day.

- *Preparation by staff and consultant experts.* Strategic planning has long been dominated by experts wielding sophisticated analytical models. Many executives see this as too abstract and remote from their concerns. They resent being isolated from much of the planning process and want to contribute to a strategy that they personally own. Jack Welch at GE dramatically reduced the company's huge planning staffs by half. Many companies have lost their love for large, lengthy, and costly strategy studies prepared by planning staffs and sold by consulting firms.

- *Detailed planning books and slide decks.* Countless managers have read their way through thick and highly specific planning books and PowerPoint presentations covering goals, budgets, financial projections, and assignments. Binders and slides are shown or e-mailed out to all managers, who are asked to comply with the recommendations. Excessively detailed plans, however, are an invitation for organizations to become lost in the trees. They provide a meticulous map to a landscape that may no longer exist.

- *Planning tied to budget goals and market projections.* Many organizations use strategic planning as the modus operandi for setting an annual budget. Yet budgets do not a strategy make. At best, they serve to allocate and account for resources once a strategy is set.

- *Planning that separates thinking from doing.* The separation between strategic thinking and doing is a false dichotomy. Executives have neither the patience nor the time to wait for lengthy data-driven studies as a prelude to action. They want to be involved early so their own opinions, judgment, and creativity can shape the discussion about strategy. Moreover, they are questioning the long-cherished assumption that implementation begins after a plan is carefully conceived. They are finding that execution starts with formulation, not with implementation. Including key stakeholders early in strategy formulation can result not only in a more realistic strategy but one that has the essential commitment needed later for effective action.

- *Strategy as a separate subject.* For years, strategy has been treated as an independent subject. Executives are finding, however, that simply addressing strategy as if it is a separate property of the organization is too idealistic. Strategy has to be considered with everything else occurring in and around the organization. If taken out of the organization context, strategy will remain at thirty thousand feet, floating in the clouds.

These conventional approaches to strategic planning thwart real-time thinking and action, and they leave participants discouraged and cynical, as suggested by McKinsey consultants Dye and Sibony (2007) who surveyed senior executives on their experiences with planning and reached this conclusion: "For the better part of a year, corporate planners collect financial and operational data, make forecasts and prepare lengthy presentations with the CEO and other senior managers about the future of the business. But at the end of this expensive and time-consuming process, many participants say they are frustrated by the lack of impact on either their own actions or the strategic direction of the company" (p. 1).

Worse yet, traditional planning can create the illusion of strategy-making without really providing the firm with a clear strategic direction. In the words of strategy guru Richard Rumelt (quoted in Lovallo and Mendonca, 2007, p. 1): "Most corporate 'strategic plans' have little to do with strategy. They are simply three-year or five-year rolling resource budgets and some market share projection. Calling it 'strategic planning' creates false expectations that the exercise will somehow produce a coherent strategy."

## CEOs Express Their Disenchantment

Not surprising, CEOs faced with rapidly changing markets are becoming disenchanted with strategic planning. A recent survey of global executives shows the magnitude of their discontent (Dye and Sibony, 2007):

- More than half of 796 respondents were dissatisfied with their strategy efforts.
- Eighty percent viewed their strategic approach as "inefficient."
- Forty-four percent said their strategic plans do not "track execution."
- Ninety percent said that organization "speed" and "agility" have become increasingly urgent issues for them over the past five years.

Our own research with CEOs shows them rejecting old-style strategic planning because of inefficiencies, long time frames, and weak connections to implementation. Consider the following interview comments from a broad sample of CEOs:

"We can't create plans that encompass and understand our global market that is so diverse and complex."

"Our markets are being upset daily by continuous cost cutting and outsourcing to Asian manufacturers, which makes any planning seem ridiculous."

"We're living only in the short term—there is no long term because of quarterly demands from investors and analysts for immediate results."

"Our industry has been wracked by acquisitions and takeovers that make us live only for daily survival. I could be gone tomorrow."

"We paid millions to a strategy consulting firm, and by the time it reported back, the market opportunities were gone."

"I feel like a football coach: 'Win now or you're fired.'"

"I don't know anyone today who has ever completed a five-year plan with one-year updates, which has long been the model."

"How can one rationally plan for irrational events?"

Many CEOs are casualties of this turmoil; one indication is the low median tenure of CEOs (five and a half years) in S&P 500 companies for 2006 (Spencer Stuart study, 2007). There is no honeymoon for CEOs to sit around to study the situation or call in a consultant for a year-long study. They have little time to initiate strategic planning or implement it so that it is accepted by the workforce. Their actions and results are being scrutinized from the outset, and their successors, whether insider or outsider, fail to affect performance up or down (Greiner and Bhambri, 1989).

## The Search for Alternatives

For these concerned executives and many others, the competitive environment is too complex and full of surprises for conventional strategic planning to anticipate. Market forces that do not bend easily to the certainty of formal planning have turned their plan-ning world upside down. Consequently they search elsewhere for solutions to speed up decisions and respond to changing events, often relying on their own hunches and ideas about strategic planning. But some solutions are more apparent than real.

## Pseudo Strategy-Making

This can result in pseudo strategy-making, which consists of palliatives that are temporary, reactive, and superficial. These alternative methods tend to neglect or simplify the substance of strategy: how the firm will achieve and sustain competitive advan-tage in a particular industry, place, and time. Among the most popular alternatives to traditional strategic planning are these:

- *Let politics determine strategy.* In this alternative, key stake-holders exercise power in a political game to determine who will dictate firm strategy. The result has more to do with the organization's power dynamics and executives' personalities than strategy. Because there are winners and losers in the influence game, competition, compromise, and accommodation influence strategy-making more than the competitive environment does.

- *Rely on annual budget and operating plan.* The focus here is on beating past results: "Let's do 10 percent better than last year on revenues and lower costs by 5 percent." In this approach, financial numbers drive a company's strat-egy, the focus is on short-term goals, controls, and budgets rather than the marketplace. In the absence of a substan-tive strategy, annual exhortations from senior management to boost the top line and cut expenses are often hollow rhetoric.

- *Expect the new CEO to be a savior.* This white-knight approach to strategy relies on a new, charismatic CEO to revitalize the firm. It is the fastest way to come up with a new strategy: the CEO creates the strategy and implements it through the top management team. This often happens in entrepreneurial companies, but it will likely fail in larger, more formal companies where many people have to own and execute the strategy. Because they are insulated, CEOs often lack the knowledge and information they need to make informed strategic decisions. Jack Welch at GE and Lou Gerstner at IBM were successful exceptions, but they were also outstanding at discussion, feedback, and keeping strategy simple and motivating.

- *Set a vision.* CEOs typically have visions, grounded in intuition, about where they want to take the organization in the future. In addition, consultants and staff experts have developed vision-setting workshops where top management meets and talks about what it ideally wants the company to become. More often than not, this results in clichés and slogans rather than substantive statements about the marketplace and the economics necessary for successful strategy. These give rise to broad catchphrases, like "the customer comes first" or "make a quality product," that are intended to inform and inspire employees. These slogans typically appear on plaques, posters, Web sites, and plastic cards. And that's where they remain, rarely communicating strategic substance or showing how to translate strategy into action.

- *Let tactics equal strategy.* Here, executives hope that short-term, ad hoc decisions and actions will somehow add up to a coherent strategy. For example, they lurch reactively from one problem to the next, based on market demands or intuition rather than a clear strategic direction. They send managers out to act as entrepreneurs looking for and attempting to exploit unique opportunities that appear.

They mistake acquisitions for a growth strategy. Unfortunately, most acquisitions don't work out, especially when they are large and unrelated to the core business and not integrated well into the firm (Buono and Bowditch, 2003). All of these decisions and actions are more tactical than strategic and can lead to a very chaotic and fragmented strategy.

- *Decentralize planning.* Top management shifts the burden of strategic planning to lower-level units where knowledge about markets exists. But these subunit leaders usually stumble over the same issues that perplex senior management. They are expected to develop local strategies where there is no overall corporate strategy to help guide them. This often results in parochial decisions that are suboptimal for the overall firm.

These methods of pseudo strategy-making may be timely, simple, and action oriented, but their effectiveness is temporary and superficial at best. They tend to be one-off attempts that lack coherence, comprehensiveness, and continuity. Many are limited to the senior management team, with little participation or involvement from the wider organization. Most don't produce realistic or implementable results, and they fizzle after a lot of fanfare. Few, if any, produce a clear and sustainable strategy over time.

## A More Substantial Approach

As we have shown, traditional strategic planning is ill suited to today's 24/7 world, and efforts to substitute pseudo approaches are just that. Thus, many executives are puzzled and confused about how to proceed.

New, dynamic approaches to strategy-making are needed so organizations can respond coherently and rapidly to fast-paced environments. Coherence means strategy must be enacted in a unified way by everyone in the firm, not just limited to top management. All employees must understand the strategy so they can respond on the spot and become the glue that holds the business together. Speed means that strategy must become real-time in both formation and execution: its content must be constantly adjusted to fit changing conditions, and its implementation must be a continuous process of translating the strategy into immediate and relevant action.

In the following chapters, you will see how *dynamic strategy-making* enables an organization to create, reshape, and execute strategy around the clock and every day. *Dynamic strategy-making* is sustainable and readily revised as events dictate and initiatives are accomplished. It also permeates the entire organization so members behave real-time on a daily basis, in alignment with a strategic direction that is created and maintained through high involvement practices from the outset.

*Dynamic strategy-making* is a practical approach to setting and executing strategy on time and with ongoing revision in response to changing events. In the following chapters, we avoid universal dictums with vague implications for practice and instead give more useful guidelines and methods that organizations can tailor to their own situations. *Dynamic strategy-making* derives from our own research and consulting practice, as well as from the rapidly expanding knowledge in strategy and organizations. It offers a road map for navigating today's strategy-making terrain, while recognizing that the journey's success rests ultimately with organization members' skills, commitment, and teamwork.

## Upcoming Chapters

Chapter Two, "Lessons from Experience," which draws on our own consulting, presents some lessons and guiding principles underlying *dynamic strategy-making*. Chapter Three, "Lessons from Strategy Knowledge," describes lessons derived from the strategy literature that serve as the scientific foundation for *dynamic strategy-making*.

Chapter Four, "Building a Strategic System," provides an overview of *dynamic strategy-making*, which involves constructing a dynamic strategic system that can address both strategic content and strategic process in real time—the what and how of strategy-making.

The next two chapters describe the strategic content part of strategy-making. Chapter Five, "Making a Strategic Assessment," provides an analytical framework, the 4D framework, to guide managers through making an assessment of the organization and its competitive environment. It identifies external sources of competitive advantage and how well the firm's internal capabilities align with them. Based on this strategic analysis, Chapter Six, "Crafting a Strategic Statement," shows how to prepare and write a statement of strategic direction. It provides a concrete format for recording and continually updating strategic content over time.

The next two chapters describe the strategic process part of strategy-making. Chapter Seven, "Using Guided Involvement," explains how to organize and stimulate discussion among managers as they create strategy and act on it. It gives step-by-step guidelines on how to engage managers in constructive dialogue so they can share their views of strategic content, listen to each other, and arrive at sufficient consensus about where the organization should be headed and how it will get there. It also gives some pointers about extending involvement to the entire workforce because the new strategic system must permeate the organization.

Chapter Eight, "Leading, Changing, and Following-Up in Real Time," explains that strategic leadership and change are essential to launching and guiding *dynamic strategy-making*. It describes how leaders can start the strategy-making process and constantly monitor, reinforce, and revise it—keeping it sustainable into the future. Chapter Nine, "Facilitating Real-Time Strategy: A New Role for Consultants," talks to professional and internal consultants seeking to facilitate strategy-making. It is a new and emerging role—a combination of conventional strategy consulting and more behavior-based organization development practices. Client managers are often in the dark and must become wiser about selecting facilitative consultants instead of turning to old friends or consulting firms with brand reputations.

Chapter Ten, "Real-Time Issues FAQ," answers questions that readers might have about *dynamic strategy-making*, such as how to apply it to nonprofits and how to involve boards. Chapter Eleven, "Last Words on Underlying Themes," concludes by highlighting major themes supporting real-time strategy-making. We remind executives that they themselves, not consultants, must design and execute *dynamic strategy-making* if they are to own it as a way of life for their organizations. The guidelines offered in this book are useful when they are adapted to fit a specific organization and situation. They allow flexibility, opportunism, and responsiveness in making strategic decisions rapidly.

Appendixes A, B, and C narrate three detailed research case studies contributing to our perspective on strategy-making. Lessons from all of them are derived in Chapter Two. The first two were strategic failures that provided us with much early learning about strategy. The third was a strategic success from our initial involvement in *dynamic strategy-making*. The executive team in this last case taught us a great deal, from which we went on to clarify our thinking and methodology; we refer to the case more fully in subsequent chapters. Following that experience, we learned further from many consulting engagements in large and small organizations ranging across industries, including manufacturing, service and high tech, along with several nonprofits. Appendix D contains an example of strategic statement from Johnson & Johnson referred to in Chapter Six.

# 2

# LESSONS FROM EXPERIENCE

*Dynamic strategy-making* derives from our own research and consulting experience, as well as from emergent knowledge about strategy. In this chapter, we focus on nine lessons from our own thirty years of experience in working with and studying organizations; in Chapter Three, we add four more lessons from historical and emerging research on strategy. Many experts have characterized strategy-making as a combination of art and science, where managers rely on judgment and knowledge. Chapter Two is more about the art, and Chapter Three is more about the science. These lessons provide the material from which we built our own real-time approach to formulating and executing strategy in an ever changing world.

## Learning from Case Research and Clients

Our experience with corporate strategy grew out of earlier work with organizations in managing change. We both started our academic and consulting careers in the 1960s from a perspective acquired through our training in organization development and change, which at the time emphasized open communication, good interpersonal relations, and employee participation as paths to organization success.

By the 1980s, our research and consulting experience increasingly pointed to larger factors such as organization design and corporate strategy as key determinants of how well firms competed and performed. We regularly observed that failing organizations were ineffective at making and executing strategy, especially in changing conditions. Corporate strategy was either missing altogether or too vague and misunderstood to provide a clear direction. Moreover, even when strategy was clear, the linkage between formulation and execution was often missing. Organizations lacked effective methods for translating strategy into relevant action.

Thus, our research and consulting evolved toward strategy-making. We focused mainly on understanding the practice of strategy-making and developing useful methods for improving it. We have been fortunate to study and work with a wide range of organizations seeking to formulate and implement strategy: manufacturing and service companies, domestic and global corporations, those in low- and high-tech industries, the public sector, and nonprofit organizations. In one way or another, we increasingly noticed that many of them faced highly competitive, ever changing environments that demanded rapid and continuous choices about strategy. Traditional methods of strategy-making had let them down, and they sought alternative approaches more suited to the new, uncertain world with many surprises.

We describe the lessons we learned from studying and working with these organizations. In many ways, they were our teachers; they taught us the art side of how to do real-time strategy-making more effectively. The lessons are illustrated in three case studies that we developed for purposes of research, to understand better what contributed to their outcomes. To ensure that each case was factual and objective, two researchers gathered data and wrote up the cases. Each case is presented in synopsis form, and all are described at greater length in the appendixes to this book. The first two cases, Coast Yellow Pages and Gamma Bank, were strategic failures that we had the opportunity to study as authors and researchers.

The third case, Petrofuels Energy, depicts successful, real-time strategy-making at a company where one of us served as a consultant facilitator. This case is both art and science. It provides a rare look at a management team effectively developing and implementing a dynamic strategy in real time with the help of concepts. Our Petrofuels experience occurred early in the development of our model of *dynamic strategy-making* and richly allowed us to learn by doing. We refer to all three cases, and other examples, throughout this book.

## Case 1: Coast Yellow Pages

A new CEO, Jack Anderson, entered with a personal vision to transform Coast Yellow Pages (CYP) from a paper-based advertising firm into a global, electronic information company—a precursor to Google. Anderson, previously a management consultant, had recently been in charge of strategic planning for the parent telephone company. To jump-start CYP's conversion, Anderson immediately added several outsiders to his management team. He briefly mentioned his long-term vision during the hiring process, but never held in-depth discussions on future strategy with the management team.

In joining CYP, Anderson encountered a highly bureaucratic company with functional silos and a steep hierarchy. It was viewed as a cash cow by its parent: its profits were equal to those firms in the top fifty of the Fortune 100. The sales force was unionized and highly paid based on how much business each salesperson brought in under a rich incentives scheme. CYP had long held a captive market in a large region, so sales were easily made by simply appearing at a customer's door. Deregulation was rapidly bringing new competition to the region, however.

Just prior to Anderson's arrival, the vice president of marketing developed a plan to rescope the yellow pages directory in the firm's biggest market: several new community directories to serve different ethnic and community groups would now accompany the main directory. Anderson asked for a presentation of the business case for the plan so he could review and approve it. What Anderson did not know was that the case contained cooked numbers that were inflated to make things look good. Anderson approved the project based on these misleading market data and even boosted its goals. He added a new performance target of 32 percent increase in revenues over the prior year, plus a change in sales compensation to reflect this new goal. The sales force would continue to be paid for new accounts but at a lower payout schedule in the initial months of selling than previously. Anderson got union officials to agree to these changes.

Once the plan went into effect, however, the sales force went on a "blue flu" strike because of the delayed and lower payments for sales; by then, revenues were far short of meeting the 32 percent goal. Anderson quickly met with the sales force to reinforce the new plan and solicit feedback. Despite hearing a lot of complaining and sounding off, he resolved to press ahead and add more salespeople to recapture lost sales. This was accomplished by decentralizing responsibility to middle managers to create several new sales groups composed of outside salespeople to call on customers, especially in the ethnic communities. Sales did improve and were higher than the year before, but they still were far short of plan. Anderson nevertheless declared the rescope project a success and remained strongly committed to pursuing his vision.

Over the next several months, Anderson's new strategy failed to gain much support in the firm, especially from the sales force that was essential to its implementation. Subsequently he lost favor with the parent company and the CYP board, after high turnover in its membership, would not provide the capital needed to execute his vision. Shortly afterward, Anderson left CYP.

At least two key lessons can be drawn from this case, both having to do with strategy content and strategic change.

### Lesson 1
Leaders need to have sufficient power and credibility to initiate strategic change and move the organization forward.

Power and credibility typically come from a strong support network and a proven track record of successful changes.

Anderson had neither of these at CYP. His top management team was new and had limited connections in the firm; moreover, none of them knew that the marketing projections were inflated. In addition, the problem-ridden project had severely damaged Anderson's credibility as a change agent. Rather than make small changes early to gain credibility, he chose to make major changes in CYP's largest market coupled with other changes in pay, a sure recipe for big trouble.

Appendix A contains a more in-depth case study of Coast Yellow Pages.

### Lesson 2
The practicality and timing of a new strategy should be examined and debated carefully by all relevant stakeholders early in the strategy-making process.

## Case 2: Gamma Bank

Gamma Bank, a major financial institution, sought outside help to address motivational issues among its branch employees. A prominent consultant visited the bank and gave a presentation to senior executives about improving motivation. The consultant later characterized the meeting as a "political zoo," with several executives heatedly disagreeing with each other.

Within weeks, Gamma reversed course and decided that its problem was "strategy," not motivation, so it quickly hired a blue-chip consulting firm to do a strategy study and put two key executives in charge of the study project: the president of the retail banking division and the executive vice president of the wholesale banking division. But both had trouble scheduling subsequent study project meetings with the consultants: they were never able to be in the same room at the same time with the consultants. It was well known at Gamma that the two executives didn't care much for each other and did not respect their boss, Gamma's chairman/CEO who was nearing retirement. Both very much wanted his job.

Halfway through the strategy study project, a troubling incident occurred at the local airport when the lead consultant came upon the chairman/CEO who offered the consultant a ride back into town. During the ride, the consultant told the chairman/CEO that the bank "would not make its budget projections during the quarter at hand," which was close to ending. The chairman/CEO was upset and the next day called in the president and executive vice president to ask for an explanation. Both denied that the budget would not be met. After the meeting, the president called the consulting firm and requested that it remove the consultant from the project, and it did.

At the end of the study project, the consultants made recommendations for Gamma's future strategy, which were well received by the bank's top twenty executives. Their report did not include suggestions for implementing the new strategy, however. So approval was sought and given for a second study on implementation for a large fee. The consulting firm treated strategy analysis as separate from implementation, which was an add-on service to generate more revenue.

Six weeks into the implementation study, to the surprise of the consultants, Gamma's largest shareholder from Europe sent a new CEO to take charge of the bank. He informed the consultants that he was interested in hearing what they had to say but should wait until he got settled. Four weeks later, he fired both the president and the executive vice president but kept the chairman/CEO. Two months later, the bank was sold to an acquirer. The implementation study was never completed.

We learned three key lessons from studying Gamma that would later guide development of *dynamic strategy-making*.

### Lesson 3
The longer the strategy-making process, the more susceptible it is to unanticipated disruptions.

In fast-paced environments, a lot can happen quickly to render strategy-making outdated and irrelevant. Gamma's lengthy strategy studies could not keep pace with the political dynamics and changes occurring in the organization and in its relations to external stakeholders. A shorter strategy process is less likely to encounter such disruptions. And even if it does, the costs should be smaller than those of a more lengthy process.

### Lesson 4
Strategy formulation and implementation are inextricably connected and should be considered at the same time.

The choice of strategic direction should be closely tied to what an organization is capable of implementing. Treating formulation and implementation in sequential steps, as the consultants did at Gamma, can lead to strategy choices that are unrealistic and troublesome, if not impossible to execute.

### Lesson 5
Key stakeholders need to be actively involved in strategy-making from its outset to resolve any substantive differences or political conflicts among them.

Gamma's strategy-making process was dominated by external consultants with little involvement from key executives or external stakeholders. It provided scant opportunity for the senior executives to address and work through their differences or the European shareholder to voice its opinion. Because ownership and commitment to the process rested mainly with the consultants, strategy-making became disconnected from the realities facing the client organization.

Appendix B contains a fuller case study of Gamma Bank.

## Case 3: Petrofuels Energy

Petrofuels Energy, a large nationwide distributor of fuels to many businesses and households, embarked on a unique and successful strategic change process led by new CEO Wil Martin, a former consultant and air force pilot. Martin had inherited a capable top management team, so he did not replace any senior managers. Because Petrofuels competed in a mature commodity market, Martin wanted to explore moving the firm in a more growth-oriented direction. Petrofuels distributed different types of fuel, ranging from aircraft to propane, to businesses and residences across the United States.

Martin soon discovered to his surprise, however, that Petrofuels was 25 percent behind its annual budget goal with five months remaining. So rather than focus on strategy, he asked his team to consider ways to make the budget. He proposed raising prices because it would have an immediate effect on the bottom line. The team resisted this idea, fearing Petrofuels would lose customers. But in a bold move, Martin asked team members to "trust me," and they agreed to go along with the price rise, betting that customers would not leave them in this short time frame.

At the end of three months, Petrofuels exceeded the budget goals, and Martin rewarded his team with bonuses and gold clocks to symbolize "excelling under time pressure." This quick success contributed to Martin's leadership credibility and power in the firm. It also provided good momentum for strategy-making.

Martin then hired two of his former professors, one of them, Larry Greiner, to facilitate the strategy process. The consultants first interviewed members of the senior team using a SWOT (strength/weakness/opportunity/threat) format and then, with Martin's help, designed a series of three off-site workshops over eight weeks to address strategy issues. The first workshop began with feedback from the consultants about what they had learned in the interviews. The team generally agreed with the conclusions and clarified some points. Initially, however, team members did not see the need to come up with a new strategy for Petrofuels because they believed that their main task was to generate cash from current operations to pay off annual interest on their parent firm's large debt. Martin persuaded them to go ahead, saying, "We have to take control over our destiny."

Next, the consultants divided the team into two subgroups and asked each to identify strategic options for Petrofuels. Martin, saying "I don't want to dominate," rotated among the two subgroups. Only two strategic alternatives emerged for debate: to diversify into other household products, like extermination, and into services, like pipeline and tank repair, that Petrofuels could sell to its current customers or focus solely on fuels. The consultants then asked the subgroups to discuss the strengths and weaknesses of the current organization and propose ways to improve it. Some members argued to restructure Petrofuels around product groups, while others preferred the existing functional structure. Then one member spoke up: "We can't settle the organization until we settle the strategy." All agreed.

The strategy discussion resumed with the consultants asking participants to address each of the two options in terms of its value proposition. The ensuing dialogue revealed a new insight for how Petrofuels could achieve competitive advantage: remain focused on the fuel business but build off existing strengths, such as outcompeting small, inefficient suppliers by providing better delivery service and assured safety. Customers might be willing to pay a few cents more per gallon in return for these features, since they depended on fuel for immediate needs, ranging from refueling airplanes to home heating and cooking. The team also suggested selling off nonfuel assets and exiting low-profit markets. Martin concluded the discussion saying, "I could get excited about that strategy and goal."

As preparation for the next workshop, each member was asked to write a concise statement of strategic direction and send it to one person, who would combine them into a final draft on behalf of the team. They also needed to review their statements with their own management teams. At the workshop, team members enthusiastically approved the following draft strategy statement that described a new direction for the company:

> Petrofuels is a leading marketer and distributor of fuels to a broad range of customers at the retail and wholesale levels. We set aggressive financial goals and achieve growth through

market development and acquisitions. Our people establish a competitive advantage in selected market segments through a unified effort that demands:

- A strong marketing orientation
- High standards of safety
- Outstanding service "before our customers need us"

Many of these features did not exist in the current company. The team also added a financial goal of "doubling sales and profits in five years" and created a banner with the rallying cry, "Double in five."

At the final workshop, team members specified strategic initiatives and action steps to implement the new strategy. This included reorganizing the company so it was better prepared to deliver service and make acquisitions. Thirty-eight managers changed jobs within the firm. To ensure a high level of service and safety, delivery drivers were trained and supplied with repainted or new trucks. A profit-sharing plan with the workforce was implemented. In addition, a plan for communicating and discussing the practical implications of the new strategy with the workforce was created; it included a big employee celebration with managers giving their personal views on the new strategy and goals, as well as Wil Martin visiting all the terminals to discuss the strategy and answer questions.

During the next two years, Petrofuels more than doubled its financial results, far exceeding the five-year target. Many employees, feeling empowered to make decisions, took on added responsibilities in the company. With continued success and updates to the strategy, Petrofuels was eventually sold at the end of six years for a high multiple of its original value. In the selling contract, all employees who desired to stay with Petrofuels had to be retained by the acquirer for up to two years.

Because Petrofuels was one of our first experiences in helping organizations do real-time strategy-making, it provided the main impetus for further development of our approach to strategy-making. Petrofuels's managers taught us a great deal about analyzing strategy and how to organize a retreat discussion. In so doing, we invented methods along the way that met their needs. They taught us that it takes more than one retreat to develop a strategy, that it should be written down briefly and concisely, and to follow up with celebrations and other involvement activities.

### Lesson 6
Strategy process (the how and who of strategy-making) has a strong influence on strategy content (the what of strategy-making).

At Petrofuels, we came to realize that who you put in the room and how you design the process for formulating strategy makes a big difference in final content. The senior executives had strong and often conflicting opinions about the business and where it should be heading. The workshops' design and facilitation promoted member participation and open dialogue, which enabled members to work through their differences and achieve consensus around a new strategy.

We continue to be impressed by how executives like those at Petrofuels excel in developing the content of viable, real-time strategies. Clearly the process helps them create the content. As consultant facilitators, we continue to help clients with organized workshops, provide concepts to analyze, and offer a format to record their strategic thinking. While strategies created this way may not be viewed by outside experts as ideal in the absence of additional data and analysis from studies, we found that execution is more assured when executives gain consensus and personal ownership of a new strategy. We have witnessed lots of consultant strategy projects that are strong on data and analysis but weak on achieving sufficient commitment for implementation.

### Lesson 7
In addition to a market and economic focus, strategy-making involves related issues having to do with strategic goals, organization values and design, and initiatives and action steps.

Like many other scholars and practitioners at the time, we viewed strategy rather narrowly, mainly in terms of market and economic focus. The Petrofuels team awakened us to a much broader perspective. Members discussed and made choices about what product or service features would win over customers (later we called these "customer tiebreakers"), financial goals, celebration goals (we later called these "rallying" goals), corporate values, organization structure, and initiatives with action steps. All of these were essential strategy issues; they were an integral part of choosing the right strategy and implementing it effectively.

### Lesson 8
Strategy is easier to communicate and understand when its content is written down in a clear, concrete, and brief form.

Petrofuels's team wanted the content of its newly created strategy to be written down clearly and concisely to avoid misinterpretation at a verbal level when leaving the workshop to communicate with other employees. Members had previous experience with lengthy strategy statements that ended up neither communicating strategy nor getting it implemented. They also wanted all their words captured on a single page. This led us to develop and refine what we have come to call a *statement of strategic direction* to capture the outcomes of strategy-making.

### Lesson 9
Active CEO leadership matters a great deal in strategy-making.

Wil Martin's leadership skills and credibility were critical in moving the process along at Petrofuels. We initially thought that our facilitation skills would be sufficient in that regard; however, the top team was more sensitive to what its boss was saying than to us. This enabled Martin to make a number of critical interventions that we couldn't have made.

## Nine Lessons and Counting

Hands-on learning at Petrofuels Energy, Gamma Bank, and Coast Yellow Pages, as well as subsequent clients, helped us to discover which methods facilitate or fail to support real-time strategy-making. Exhibit 2.1 (on the following page) summarizes the lessons derived from our experience—the art of strategy. Chapter Three gleans more lessons from the strategy literature of theories and research, the science of strategy, which has progressed greatly over the years.

# Exhibit 2.1 Nine Lessons from Experience

*Lesson 1*: Leaders need to have sufficient power and credibility to initiate strategic change and move the organization forward.

*Lesson 2*: The practicality and timing of a new strategy should be examined and debated carefully by all relevant stakeholders early in the strategy-making process.

*Lesson 3*: The longer the strategy-making process, the more susceptible it is to unanticipated disruptions.

*Lesson 4*: Strategy formulation and implementation are inextricably connected and should be considered at the same time.

*Lesson 5*: Key stakeholders need to be actively involved in strategy-making from its outset to resolve any substantive differences or political conflicts among them.

*Lesson 6*: Strategy process (the how and who of strategy-making) has a strong influence on strategy content (the what of strategy-making).

*Lesson 7*: In addition to a market and economic focus, strategy-making involves related issues having to do with strategic goals, organization values and design, and initiatives and action steps.

*Lesson 8*: Strategy is easier to communicate and understand when its content is written down in a clear, concrete, and brief form.

*Lesson 9*: Active CEO leadership matters a great deal in strategy-making.

# 3

# LESSONS FROM STRATEGY KNOWLEDGE

In this chapter, we summarize the main lessons we have learned from strategy research and show how these scientific lessons helped us to develop *dynamic strategy-making*. Scientific strategy research and knowledge have been and are growing enormously, offering useful but often indirect advice about strategy-making. Unfortunately, executives and other practitioners often find it hard to access or apply this knowledge. Much of the information is couched in academic terms and models that are too abstract for particular situations or too complex for practical application.

Mintzberg, Lampel, and Ahlstrand (1998) provided an earlier and more extensive summary of the strategy literature in *Strategy Safari* than we present, but they did not divide it into phases and with the same lessons as we do here. By interpreting and reframing this research and pointing out the lessons of each phase, we hope to make it clear and more useful to strategy-makers. The evolving strategy knowledge can be organized into four distinct temporal phases that overlap and build on each other, offering useful lessons for *dynamic strategy-making*:

Before 1975: Business Policy and Executive Judgment

1970–1990: Market Position and Competitive Advantage

1985–1995: Core Competence and Resource Based

1990–today: Leadership and Execution

To these we will add a fifth phase for what we think comes next.

## Before 1975: Business Policy and Executive Judgment

The serious intellectual study of business strategy began in 1938 with the publication of Chester Barnard's classic book, *Functions of the Executive*. It emphasized that organizational effectiveness requires constant adaptation to a firm's environment. However, it wasn't until after World War II, with its emphasis on military strategy, that corporate strategy took on momentum with the first strategy course at the Harvard Business School called "business policy" (Cruikshank, 1987). This course became the capstone for the Harvard M.B.A. program, drawing on and integrating all the preceding courses in the business disciplines.

Case discussions, the dominant pedagogy, emphasized three key assumptions about strategy-making: (1) senior executives are responsible for strategy—for setting the objectives and policies to move the company forward; (2) strategy-making relies on managerial analysis, judgment, and action; and (3) each firm's strategic problems are unique, requiring a specific strategy to fit the situation. Consequently, business leaders need to have the necessary diagnostic skills for assessing a company's capabilities and opportunities, the essential judgment for making wise strategic choices, and the practical social skills for implementing a strategy geared to a specific firm. All of this led to the writing of many cases for textbooks (Learned, Christensen, Andrews, and Guth, 1969).

This view of strategy soon spread to business education and management consulting throughout the world affecting many executives and organizations. It also spawned popular analytical tools such as the SWOT framework, invented by Al Humphrey at Stanford, which helps executives assess their situation and invent solutions to fit their competitive environment. This proliferation of strategic thinking was the beginning of the next phase, leading to the emergence of strategy as a legitimate topic for scientific inquiry and research (Andrews, 1971).

This first phase provides a key lesson that is as relevant for strategy-making today as it was in earlier times:

### Lesson 10
Senior executives, using their own experience, expertise, and judgment, are responsible for creating and executing a unique strategy for their firms.

We are constantly amazed at how often top leaders seem to ignore this simple but profound dictum. Rather than actively leading the strategy-making effort, they relegate it to corporate staff, external consultants, or middle managers. They essentially abdicate their strategy-making role.

## 1970-1990: Market Position and Competitive Advantage

This second phase was marked by more scientific approaches to strategy-making and the rise of staff experts and large consulting firms devoted to strategy. Starting with George Steiner's research on long-range planning (Steiner, 1979), this period saw the development of a host of sophisticated models for understanding strategy-making, such as the Boston Consulting Group's (BCG) growth-share matrix and experience curve models (Henderson, 1982) and McKinsey's useful 7-S framework (Rasiel and Friga, 2002). These efforts fueled an explosion of economic and marketing concepts for analyzing a firm's competitive situation. Michael Porter's research on achieving competitive advantage through the analysis of market forces became the intellectual cornerstone of this period (Porter, 1980, 1985).

These models emphasized competitive features outside the firm that attract and retain customers, like price, quality, and service. The concept of market inefficiencies, for example, pointed companies toward niches where they could win through greater efficiency and service. The frameworks also showed companies how to manage portfolios of businesses, thus fueling the growth of diversification, mergers, and acquisitions. Even marketing research became strategic, explaining how companies could enhance products not only to attract customers but to protect them from competitors' goods and services.

On the practical side, companies used this increased knowledge to mitigate the risk of strategy-making. Many firms created large planning departments staffed by strategy experts; GE built a planning staff of more than two hundred, for instance, and created detailed analyses and planning books to show executives what strategies they should pursue. These developments also fueled the growth of major strategy consulting firms, such as BCG, Bain, and Monitor, which sold large contracts to analyze a company's competitive situation using their proprietary models.

We distill from this second stage the following important learning for today's strategy-making:

Lesson 11
Seek a market position or opportunity where the firm uses a combination of unique features to attract customers in ways that competitors can't easily match.

## 1985-1995: Core Competence and Resource Based

This era saw strategy research move internally to identify which of the organization's capabilities and resources could best lead to competitive advantage (Ulrich and Lake, 1990). This filled a gap missing in the previous, externally focused phase, which also had come under increasing attack for excessive market studies—analysis paralysis, as many critics labeled it. Many of the strategic planning notebooks left by consulting firms and staff planning departments were never read or implemented; they simply gathered dust on bookshelves, as the cliché goes.

The resource-based view of the firm showed that competitive advantage can accrue from organizations' building off their existing product, organizational, and technological capabilities (Wernerfelt, 1984; Barney, 1991). Acquiring new capabilities is likely too costly and inefficient. For example, nearly 80 percent of the acquisitions made during the 1970s and 1980s did not work out because they were unrelated to the acquiring firm's core products and other resources (Buono and Bowditch, 2003). Transaction cost economics explained how to improve competitive advantage by reducing the inefficiencies occurring as products and services pass along the firm's value chain (Williamson, 1991). Practical efforts to make the chain more efficient included various business process and financial reengineering projects (Tufano, 1996).

As a prelude to the next phase of knowledge development, this era also saw an emerging focus on the human and organizational side of strategy-making. Good leadership and talented and motivated employees were tied to strategic success. This led to a spate of best practices in leadership and human resource management (Cascio, 1986).

Identifying and matching an organization's resources and capabilities to market opportunities requires careful analysis and a lot of creativity. It's a serious challenge to discover and match a unique capability or resource to fit with a specific market opportunity. This leads to the following key learning for strategy-making today:

> Lesson 12
> Focus the firm on identifying specific capabilities and resources that fit certain market opportunities so as to gain competitive advantage.

## 1995-Today: Leadership and Execution

This current phase includes more dynamic views of how executives and members behave in resolving the issues mentioned above as they make and implement strategic decisions. Descriptive research has shown that strategy-making can be a lengthy incremental process involving power dynamics and conflicts of interest among key stakeholders. Strategy decisions often emerge from political compromises and tactical decisions that produce a new strategic direction over time. These decisions often reside in the personal agendas of managers (Pettigrew, 1985). Complementing this point of view is agency theory, which points to conflicts spawned out of the self-interest of senior managers who are trying to maximize gain for themselves versus the interests of shareholders (Jensen, 1994).

In contrast, other research and writing suggested that politics can be neutralized and strategic change accelerated by bringing in a new charismatic leader whose sheer willpower, motivation, and new vision shape changes in strategy-making. Jack Welch at GE and Lou Gerstner at IBM have been repeatedly lauded for rapidly changing their firms' strategic fortunes. Welch sold off businesses that were marginal to GE's core, set goals in line with the new strategy, and got employees involved in implementation with programs like WorkOut and Six Sigma (Bartlett and Wozny, 2000; Welch and Byrne, 2001). Gerstner transformed IBM from hardware into an information services company; he was also known for going out to meet with customers to learn more about the market and reactions to IBM products (Gertsner, 2002).

This era saw a special emphasis on human motivation and technology in strategy execution (Pfeffer, 1998). Many strategy consulting firms began to work closely with managers on tactical studies, such as the design and implementation of new information and compensation systems, with consultant teams moving into companies for lengthy periods of time to support strategy implementation; a good example is the balanced scorecard approach (Kaplan and Norton, 1996). Recently these viewpoints have become known as "strategy as practice," a domain of study where the focus is on the doing of strategy (Johnson, Langley, Melin, and Whittington, 2007). Other practice-oriented scholars have developed methods to involve employees in creating and implementing strategy, such as visioning (Ronis, 2007), open space (Owen, 1997), appreciate inquiry (Cooperrider, Sorenson,

Whitney, and Yeager, 2005), and future search (Weisbord and Janoff, 1995). The common belief in these models was that organizational members will not own and implement a strategy unless they are actively involved in creating it. Moreover, because managements can easily get bogged down in politics and resistance to change, involvement must be carefully organized and guided to overcome these behaviors.

Thus, all of these methods, while frequently short on strategic substance, showed how they were designed to short-circuit the political process and overcome resistance, going on to identify the positive strengths of the firm and speed up strategic decision making through interaction among the key players. Conceptual and substantive backing for this approach is found in *Blue Ocean Strategy* (Kim and Mauborgne, 2005), which advocates a reconstructionist approach in place of institutional structuralist economic concepts. According to the authors in defining the two viewpoints:

> The structuralist view (or environmental determinism) often leads to competition-based strategic thinking. Taking market structure as given, it drives companies to try to carve out a defensible position against the competition in an existing market space. Reconstructionist thinking recognizes that structure and market boundaries exist only in managers' minds; practitioners who hold this view do not let existing market structures limit their thinking [pp. 210–211].

We accept both points of view. The structuralist approach, supported by the earlier lessons, is a reality of competition and markets that exist globally today. We also recognize the reconstructionist viewpoint, in that managers can go on the offense by rapidly creating new strategies through organized discussion that are responsive to fast-paced markets. These concepts and methods lead to the following key learning and lesson from this period:

### Lesson 13
Strategy-making occurs more rapidly and effectively when the firm's senior management intervenes through leadership and

guided involvement with processes to motivate employees, promote commitment, resolve conflicts, and overcome individual
self-interest, political behavior, and other resistance obstacles.

## Next Phase: Dynamic Strategy Systems

We believe that the next era of strategy knowledge and practice
will focus on real-time strategy-making. We call it the *dynamic
strategic systems phase* to emphasize both the changing and systemic nature of strategy-making in fast-paced environments.
Eisenhardt and Martin (2000), in a critique of resource-based
theory, call for more dynamic processes to deal with high-velocity
environments. Knowledge in this phase will need to show how
firms can make strategy more flexible, open to change, and
encompassing the organization—what recently has been referred
to as "strategy dynamics" (interview with Richard Rumelt in
Lovallo and Mendonca, 2007):

> The dynamics of strategy and performance concerns the "con-
> tent" of strategy—initiatives, choices, policies and decisions
> adopted in an attempt to improve performance, and the results
> that arise from these managerial behaviors. The dynamic model
> of the strategy process is a way of understanding how strategic
> actions occur. It recognizes that strategic planning is dynamic;
> that is, strategy-making involves a complex pattern of actions and
> reactions. It is partially planned and partially unplanned [p. 66].

Although strategy dynamics has become heavily mathemat-
ical (Warren, 2007), we are interested in the practical aspects
for turning it into management practice. From this perspective, strategy-making is an ongoing, never-ending process aimed
at continuous reassessment and reinvention (Markides, 1999).
It is made complicated by strategy "deconstruction" caused by
far-reaching changes that lead to breakdowns in the value chain,
such as technological breakthroughs, outsourcing, and the opening of new markets (Bresser, Hitt, Nixon, and Heuskel, 2000).
    New strategy knowledge also needs to show how strategy-
making can be made more systemic by embedding strategic

content into the organization's objectives, design, and culture. All of these organizational features guide and reinforce how members think and behave. By considering them together as essential elements of a strategic system, organizations can create the infrastructure and reinforcement to guide and motivate strategy-making continuously throughout the firm.

There is little in the strategy literature that has considered the concept of a strategic system; the few who have discussed "strategic systems" do so in a way that comes close to but does not resemble our concept (Porter, 1996). Always ahead of his time, Porter was likely the first to call for a system that is strategically based:

> Competitive advantage grows out of the entire system of activities. The fit among activities substantially reduces cost or increases differentiation. Beyond that, the competitive value of individual activities—or the associated skills, competencies, or resources—cannot be decoupled from the system or the strategy. . . . Positions built on systems of activities are far more sustainable than those built on individual activities. Such systems, by their very nature, are usually difficult to untangle from outside the company and therefore hard to imitate [p. 73].

Our concept of a strategic system is broader than Porter's, which is constructed rather narrowly around task activities in the value chain. We believe that a dynamic strategic system, geared to creating, executing, and revising strategy constantly, is essential for successful strategy-making. It should build off the prior lessons by placing, in a more holistic sense, strategic content into many aspects of the firm such as its goals, organization, culture, and management process. So the next lesson may look something like the following:

### Lesson 14
Key stakeholders need to develop a dynamic strategic system with the necessary processes that continuously create, revise, and embed strategic content into the firm's goals, organization, and action plans, thereby giving a firm competitive advantage.

The lessons from this chapter are summarized in Exhibit 3.1.

## From Lessons to *Dynamic Strategy-Making*

In Chapter Four, we build on the lessons of Chapters Two and Three by describing the framework to construct a dynamic strategy system. Subsequent chapters elaborate further. By *framework*, we do not mean to suggest that there is a single universal system that leads to successful strategy-making in all organizations. Actual strategic content will certainly vary depending on the organization and its competitive environment.

# Exhibit 3.1 Summary of Lessons from Chapter Three

*Lesson 10*: Senior executives, using their own experience, expertise, and judgment, are responsible for creating and executing a unique strategy for their firm.

*Lesson 11*: Seek a market position or opportunity where the firm uses a combination of unique features to attract customers in ways that competitors can't easily match.

*Lesson 12*: Focus the firm on identifying specific capabilities and resources that fit certain market opportunities so as to gain competitive advantage.

*Lesson 13*: Strategy-making occurs more rapidly and effectively when the firm's senior management intervenes through leadership and guided involvement with processes to motivate employees, promote commitment, resolve conflicts, and overcome individual self-interest, political behavior, and other resistance obstacles.

*Lesson 14*: Key stakeholders need to develop a dynamic strategic system with the necessary processes that continuously create, revise, and embed strategic content into the firm's goals, organization, and action plans, thereby creating competitive advantage.

# 4

# BUILDING A STRATEGIC SYSTEM

Guided by the lessons from Chapters Two and Three, we developed this book on *dynamic strategy-making* to help organizations and their leaders become real-time strategy-makers. In this chapter, we briefly describe our conception of a real-time strategic system, which serves as the cornerstone for delivering *dynamic strategy-making* to an organization so that it keeps up in a rapidly changing world. The absence of a dynamic strategic system that permeates the entire firm explains why, in our opinion, many organizations are not able to execute their strategies and revise them in a timely way. They continue to hold on to outdated planning and execution methods where strategy becomes lost in the trees of everyday operational problems, never reaching the workforce that needs to embrace the strategy and act it out with customers.

We begin by saying more about the recent development of systemic approaches to forming and maintaining strategy. Then we explain its main building blocks of process and content, which have to be integrated in practice where one advances the other. In *dynamic strategy-making*, key stakeholders are involved from the outset in building an effective strategic system composed of market-oriented content and sound economic fundamentals. After that, Chapters Five through Nine discuss practical methods and tools to construct, lead, and involve the workforce in the process of building and leading a real-time strategic system.

While it is a challenge initially to design and build the structure of a dynamic strategic system, once constructed, it relies on continuous maintenance through real-time processes of leadership and change to add and change content as events require, initiatives are realized, and goals are accomplished.

## Recent Progress Toward a Systems View of Strategy

The idea of a strategic system is relatively new in strategy. Traditionally, the term *system* has been used in strategy to refer to the design of information systems to help monitor and implement strategy. The National Aeronautics and Space Administration, for example, has what it calls "strategic systems planning," which is geared mainly to control and budgeting.

Systemic thinking relative to strategy can be traced to the McKinsey 7-S model (strategy, structure, systems, shared values, skills, style, staff), in which most of the seven elements are organizational and behavioral and all elements should be aligned and acting as a system to achieve strategic success (Rasiel and Friga, 2002). But 7-S is a static model, making strategy only one of several variables to be aligned. No guidance is given about how to create strategy or the process of aligning a 7-S system.

In recent years, we have seen a progression of approaches to strategy that come closer to what we have in mind, in that they talk about organizational systems in relation to strategy. But most of these approaches are short on steps and dynamics to get to their proposed ideal states. Many of them also avoid discussing the content of a strategy, and they accept strategic content as a given:

- Porter's notion (1996) is that in order to sustain competitive advantage, strategic success lies in "interdependent systems of task activities" that pervade the organization and provide coherence and direction to employee behavior. These activities integrate strategic content into the organization, but the focus is on the value chain and does not take a wider viewpoint.

- Beer and Nohria's "ideal" organizational system (2000) is broader, integrating economic value with organizational capability to deal with fast-moving events. It addresses alignment among organizational elements similar to the 7-S model while adding a real-time, dynamic view with a "plan for spontaneity and innovation." But their plan does not discuss the specific process steps necessary to formulate economic content and build it into the organization.

- In Lawler and Worley's "built-to-change" organization (2006), design elements and strategy are aligned in ways that enable a firm to strategize readily and adjust quickly to changing conditions. But like Beer and Nohria, Lawler and Worley do not discuss how to come up with strategic content behind a change-minded organization.

- In Kaplan and Norton's "strategy-focused organization" (1996), the ability to execute strategy is more important than the quality of the strategy itself. Their balanced scorecard methodology is used to prescribe how organizations can create control systems and budgets that measure strategic progress. But this is limited to a measurement system linked to strategic goals.

- Rosabeth Kanter (2008) conceives of an organization acting as a "guidance system" based on a shared understanding of corporate mission and common values, standards, and tools to coordinate and direct employee behavior strategically. But it is short on specific steps that show how to come up with strategic content.

- Nadler and Tushman (1997) build strategic content into the organization structure, but they mainly limit it to the "top layers of the organization." In doing so, they do not advocate a broader strategic system that creates strategy or discuss how to develop strategic content.

- Cynthia Montgomery (2008) views strategy-making as an "organic, adaptive, holistic and open-ended process," in contrast to an "unchanging plan that derives from an analytical left-brain exercise." Unlike the others, Montgomery does focus on strategy and dynamics, but she leaves strategic content to a process of CEO leadership and decision making.

## Progress in Terms of Real-Time Criteria

These approaches point to several essential criteria for managers to take account of when creating a system aligned with strategy so as to cope effectively with fast-paced environments:

- *Speed over delay.* Organizations constantly face new opportunities and threats that need immediate strategic action. They must fight the temptation to react slowly, gathering more information and generating and assessing more solutions.
- *Breadth over narrowness.* Unpredictable and complex conditions require expansive thinking and action. Many disciplines and stakeholders have to be considered. Strategy must be comprehensive and open to new information and innovative ideas.
- *Flexibility over rigidity.* Organizations must constantly adapt and revise strategy to fit changing situations. They must discover new solutions, adjust priorities, and reallocate resources.
- *Guidelines over details.* Rather than plan out the future in detail, firms must provide strategic guideposts within which members can respond and improvise as situations change.
- *Action over deliberation.* Organizations must make rapid decisions and take quick action. If they wait to analyze and deliberate, the world will pass them by.
- *Empowerment over autocracy.* Strategy-making must permeate the entire organization and give members the freedom

to respond to local changes. It cannot remain the sole domain of top management but must include all employees so they feel that they own and can enact it.

- *Simplicity over complexity.* So many forces are affecting organizations that members can become lost in the trees. To reduce this complexity, strategy needs to be concrete and specific so it is clearly understood and can be acted on.

- *Unity over fragmentation.* Strategy must promote consistent and integrated action throughout the firm. It must counter the tendency of organizations spread out across countries, markets, and businesses to fragment, lose coordination, and deviate from the intended strategy.

- *Continuous revision over one-shot calendar events.* The old days, where five- and ten-year plans were a prelude to rolling budgets and capital spending, are long gone. Now, the only long-range planning is for major capital expenditures. Strategizing in a 24/7 mode requires constant revision and change. The only constancy is the process and the form of determining the content.

These criteria show the strong linkage between organization and strategy. Today organizations need to be fast, flexible, and empowering if they are to create, execute, and revise strategy continually.

## Limits of Organization as Strategy

Many of the thinkers we have noted above agree with these two McKinsey consultants that the organization itself can embody strategy: "Most corporate leaders overlook a golden opportunity to create a durable competitive advantage . . . by making organizational design the heart of strategy" (Bryan and Joyce, 2007, p. 20).

Like *dynamic strategy-making*, some of these perspectives advocate an organization that is continually innovating and changing to keep pace with real-time environments. Some propose ongoing data feedback and shared learning as essential to constantly adjust the organization and its strategy to the competitive environment. We agree that concepts of constant adjustment and learning are good for promoting flexibility, openness, and acceptance of change. In fact, they are essential in a real-time environment.

Many managers, consultants, and scholars have accepted these arguments, but there is a major flaw and limitation: in our view, organizations are not strategic systems. We disagree with the conclusion that "organization design is the heart of strategy." Managers may construct fast reaction practices from empowered workers, yet the organization can still lack strategic content throughout its infrastructure and behavior; it can still fail to produce a coherent direction. Strategy is not just another variable to be aligned to the organization. Rather than saying that organization is the heart of strategy, we argue that *strategy should be the heart of the organization.* Our experience suggests that strategic content should be embedded throughout the firm, but few of the approaches we have briefly reviewed here call for strategic content to be located in the organization's goals, culture, structure, and practices. This is necessary to direct, coordinate, control, and empower employee behavior.

At Petrofuels Energy, for example, the management team used content from its statement of strategic direction to add an acquisitions group, create a new marketing department to aggressively sell the firm's services and combine supply with transportation into one department to ensure efficient delivery. They also added strategic content to goals, personnel assignments, values, and action plans.

## Our Concept of a Real-Time Strategic System

The strategic system described in this book is far more comprehensive, concrete, and pragmatic than the perspectives we have reviewed. First, it views strategy as central for permeating

## Figure 4.1 Strategy-Making Format

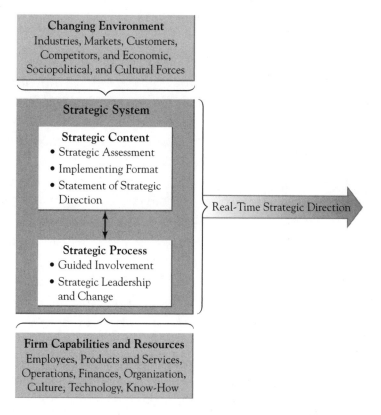

the organization rather than as simply another element to align with other parts. Second, it is both systemic and dynamic; it addresses all aspects of strategy-making: the formulation, execution, and continuous revision of strategic content. It treats process and content interactively and seeks integrative strategies that are executable and flexible. Figure 4.1 broadly outlines our framework and shows the strategic system as central and pervasive to strategy-making. The framework jointly addresses two main elements—strategic content and strategic process—in the context of continually seeking to match firm capabilities and resources (at the bottom of the figure) to changing environmental opportunities and demands (at the top) and strategic process as the involvement and leadership engine for getting there.

# Key Building Blocks: Strategic Content and Process

A strategic system must be assembled and constructed through the two key building blocks: content and process. Strategic content is the substance of strategy—what the organization intends to do to achieve a specific position and outcomes in a particular marketplace. It orients the firm in the marketplace, identifies key objectives, and guides members' behaviors. Strategic process refers to the activities and methods used to create, execute, and update strategic content. It identifies the key stakeholders involved in strategy-making and organizes and directs their interaction and decision making.

Some of the lessons in Chapters Two and Three are oriented to the content side of strategy-making (Lessons 7, 8, 11, and 12), others to its process side (Lessons 1, 3, 4, 6, and 8), and others to the stakeholders on the process side who must engage content (Lessons 2, 5, 9, 10, and 13). Lesson 14 speaks to the overall strategic system that pulls both sides together, organizing, directing, and revitalizing strategy-making.

Key stakeholders need to develop a dynamic strategic system with the necessary processes that continuously create, revise, and embed strategic content into the firm's goals, organization, and action plans, thereby creating competitive advantage.

## When Content Gets Ahead of Process, or Vice Versa

Poor results can occur when strategic content and strategic process are not tightly integrated and one gets ahead of the other. For example, content can get ahead of process. This often happens when a strategy consulting firm engages in a lengthy study conducted apart from the organization and then reports back only occasionally on its findings with a fancy slide show presentation at the end. Top management is treated as the audience. The assumption here is that intellectual insights gained from a well-executed study with lots of facts will be sufficient in themselves to convince executives about what is the best strategy. In the Coast Yellow Pages case, the CEO had a content vision to convert a paper-driven organization to an electronic information company, but he never undertook the process of gaining the board's support for his objective.

In the same way, process can get ahead of content. This typically occurs with visioning exercises in which participants meet to express their preferences for an ideal future state for their firm. These exercises often happen without sufficient attention to the realities of markets, competitors, and resources. Everyone has fun, and then it's back to business as usual. But if the vision becomes the strategy, the management team may unfortunately walk off a cliff holding hands. In the Gamma Bank case, the lead consultant told the chairman that the firm was not going to meet its budget targets, causing the chairman to call in the president and the executive vice president for an explanation; they denied it. Later, the two asked for the consultant to be removed from the project. This shows how the political process at Gamma undid the content side, and these same politics eventually resulted in the sale of the bank and the termination of the two competing partners.

## Integrating Content and Process

The challenge for strategy-making is to integrate the process with content into the strategic system from the outset. Traditionally most attention has been directed at strategic content because it is more tangible and easier to talk about than strategic process. At best, process has been an afterthought in strategy-making, if it is considered at all. Even when both content and process have been considered, they have been assigned to separate time frames and functions. Strategic content comes first and is treated as part of strategy formulation. Strategic process follows and is part of strategy implementation. This separation underlies many of the strategy execution problems we see in organizations today.

In reality, content and process are not independent activities occurring in linear sequence. Instead, they work together, each furthering the other. This is illustrated in the Petrofuels case, where an integration of process with content from the outset resulted in a strategic system accompanied by higher motivation, commitment, and greatly improved performance. Without effective processes, sound content cannot be developed. Ineffective process can cause lengthy delays in deciding on strategic content as the world passes it by or, worse, can result in choosing the wrong strategy.

## Enacting Content and Process to Form a Strategic System

Content and process have to be enacted and integrated so as to make the strategic system come alive. Organizations must weave content and process together as they construct a strategic system. To do so, tools and concepts in the form of building blocks are required to support the construction process.

### Content Building Blocks: Strategic Assessment and Written Statement

The content comes from the top managers, who are aided by analytical frameworks. Chapters Five and Six focus on the content side of *dynamic strategy-making*, with senior managers making a situational assessment through collecting, analyzing, and assessing data about the organization and its environment to inform their strategic choice. In keeping with the lessons in the preceding chapters, the firm is examined to identify core capabilities, resources, and know-how, all potential strengths needed to succeed in the marketplace.

The creative part comes into play as the environment and organization are analyzed to discover the best match between existing market opportunities and internal strengths so that the firm will gain and sustain competitive advantage. Because neither the organization nor its environment is static, this assessment is not the one-shot event so prevalent in strategy consulting but an ongoing process that is built into the organization. In fast-moving environments, the results of strategic analysis have a short shelf life, so data collection and assessment need to be continuous and keep pace with change. Chapter Five says much more about making this strategic assessment.

The content from the assessment is then transferred to a statement of strategic direction through what we call the *implementing format*, which includes four elements that compose the skeleton and anatomy of the strategic system: (1) the competitive logic composed of market position and customer tiebreakers, which provides the business model for how the organization will gain competitive advantage; (2) the strategic goals, financial and rallying, that will direct and motivate members' behavior; (3) the organization design that will structure and link members to work activities, each other, and company values; and (4) the action plan that includes strategic initiatives and specific steps for implementing the strategic system.

The statement of strategic direction provides a concrete and brief way to record, communicate, and implement the strategic system. It gives a way to avoid misunderstandings in the future and a clearer way to articulate the content with the workforce and other stakeholders about the journey ahead. Chapter Six says much more about creating the statement.

## Process Building Blocks: Guided Involvement and Strategic Leadership

Effective process rarely unfolds naturally; more often, it must be intentionally designed, guided, and led. Content will not be enacted without an effective and integrated process, which in our view involves two key processes to elicit the right content and ensure successful implementation: guided involvement and exceptional leadership.

In uncertain environments, strategic process must promote both quickness and participation. This generally requires a good deal of what we call *guided involvement*, which helps participants rapidly assess the organization and its environment, share their knowledge and experience, and agree on the strategic direction. Politics, always present, is made more constructive through guided involvement. It reaches out to all organization members to encourage their relevant participation in strategy-making and facilitate their understanding and commitment to the strategic content. Guided involvement strongly connects with strategy formulation, execution, and revision. Chapter Seven says more about how it works.

In addition, our experience suggests that strategy-making requires exceptional leadership from all managers (not just senior managers, as in the past), who act as strategic leaders across the organization. Strategic leaders must step forward and skillfully show the way to creating, executing, and refining the organization's strategy, that is, "behave strategic content" as role models and hold themselves accountable for it. This takes a good deal of vision, personal insight, and social acumen. Strategic leadership must extend from the top to the bottom of the firm. It must ensure that strategy is enacted effectively at all levels on a daily basis. This often requires change, leaving behind traditional habits and replacing them with new strategy oriented behavior. A good leader helps to make change. Chapter Eight discusses this topic in depth.

## Expanding Further on the Strategic System

The next four chapters expand on the main ideas, providing the foundation for the strategic system and offering detailed examples. Chapter Five explains strategic assessment to generate sound strategic content; Chapter Six covers transferring this content using the implementing format to the crafting of a statement of strategic direction; Chapter Seven focuses on using guided involvement to create the statement and ensure follow-up participation; and Chapter Eight emphasizes the importance of strategic leadership and change management to enable the system to become a living reality.

# 5

# MAKING A STRATEGIC ASSESSMENT

Strategic assessment by managers, aided by new knowledge and discussion, is a step toward creating content to be placed on a statement of strategic direction. This is what forms the foundation of a strategic system.

When facing new realities brought on by an ever changing world, executives can easily be blinded by their own cognitions and emotions formed through past experience. No single CEO or manager has all the answers. Some members of an executive team are wedded to the status quo and favor past practices. Under pressure, they can argue endlessly, adhering to personal past views and self-interest, often ending up by doing nothing or resorting to meaningless compromise. Furthermore, many are not aware of the strategic lessons covered in Chapters Two and Three. Hence, they stick to past practices, invent new approaches on the fly, or turn to a lengthy consulting study for help, all of which can result in dead-end solutions.

## A Fresh Look

Ways have to be found to help executives look anew at their situation so they can reach consensus with each other in creating a new strategy that will form the foundation of an enduring strategic system. This is an issue of innovating strategic content as well as using involvement: content gives the direction; involvement stimulates ideas and brings commitment to a new strategic system.

We have tried lecturing to managers about strategic knowledge, but they are inclined to reject our all-too-common scholarly assumption that answers to strategic problems lie in academic theories, which are general, not firm specific. As a result, organizations and their leaders typically rely on in-house staff or external consultants to do strategic analysis of their firm. Because these studies tend to be extensive and time-consuming, they are often too late and outdated to inform real-time strategy-making. The findings are often couched in elegant theories backed up by sophisticated data analyses, while relying on the abstract rhetoric of the consultants.

These approaches create big barriers to communication, which can make it difficult for executives to understand and agree on the findings and recommendations. The organization's world is moving too fast to wait for analysis paralysis to take its toll as events speed by them. Moreover, under these approaches, executives usually do not directly participate in collecting and analyzing data, so it is easy for them to dismiss the findings and blame the experts when preconceived notions are not met or an obvious strategy is lacking.

Strategy-making is informed through intellectual inquiry by managers about the organization and its competitive environment. This strategic assessment helps them to discover how well their capabilities and resources fit with opportunities in the environment. It provides the basis for determining strategic direction in the marketplace. Our approach to strategic assessment involves managers in real-time data collection and analysis; sort of *diagnosis on the run*. All of this is consistent with Lesson 10: Senior executives, using their own experience, expertise, and judgment, are responsible for creating and executing a unique strategy for their firm.

Key stakeholders should actively participate from the outset, so they are more likely to understand and own the findings from their analysis and commit to applying them. Members add valuable input to strategic assessment from their own experience; they possess local knowledge about the firm and its competitive

## Figure 5.1 4D Framework

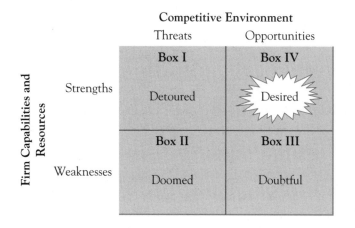

environment. This information is often unique and tacit, and not easily accessible to outsiders. It is timely and can help executives quickly revise strategies as events dictate. Our main aim is to help executives look objectively at their situation, exercise their judgments, and reach consensus on what their shared observations mean for strategic choice.

The 4D analytical framework serves many purposes, but it does not contain answers in itself—the answers emerge with use by managers. The *4D framework* helps participants look at their situation in new ways, organize and understand their experiences as they interact, and draw valid and actionable conclusions from making a strategic assessment (see Figure 5.1). We have found the 4D framework to be straightforward and understandable to managers for its practical language and implications. It stimulates and focuses discussion among members, helping them to surface and examine their strategic views and opinions, thereby enabling participants to see their situation from different perspectives, which can lead to new ideas and conclusions. In addition, the 4D framework is comprehensive and promotes an overall view of how the organization relates to its competitive environment. It promotes integration and synthesis as managers seek a coherent strategic assessment and consensus.

Built on and borrowing from the original and time-tested SWOT model, the 4D framework organizes information along two key dimensions: the first having to do with the firm's internal capabilities and weaknesses and the second with external opportunities and threats in the competitive environment. The objective is to find an external opportunity that matches up well with internal capabilities; only in this way can competitive advantage be achieved. These dimensions are consistent with Lessons 11 and 12 from Chapter Three:

> *Lesson 11*: Seek a market position or opportunity where the firm uses a combination of unique features to attract customers in ways that competitors can't easily match.

> *Lesson 12*: Focus the firm on identifying specific capabilities and resources that fit certain market opportunities so as to gain competitive advantage.

## The 4Ds

When juxtaposed, the two dimensions result in four kinds of fit between the firm's capabilities and its environment. We have labeled the four types of fit—the 4Ds of fit—but we don't explain these labels in advance to bias the managers in the retreat (the fourth of these is much more promising than the others):

- A *detoured* fit, Box I, suggests a strategy of leading from strength with the intention of countering threats. It diverts attention away from promising opportunities, as happened in AOL's acquisition of Time-Warner—two goliaths with very different business models and cultures, each trying to use its own strengths to counter a threat from the other. The benefits never materialized.

- A *doomed* fit, Box II, implies a strategy of leading from weakness to fight off threats. It is likely to end in failure, as in the case of Sears trying to challenge Wal-Mart and Costco.

- The *doubtful* fit, Box III, implies a strategy of leading from weakness to pursue opportunities, as when e-Bay, even from a strong base, entered Asia with weak local knowledge. e-Bay struggled in Japan, China, and Korea, resulting in criticism that its own arrogance led it to believe that its strengths at home would extend to the Asian market.

- The *desired* fit, Box IV, implies a strategy of aiming strengths at external opportunities that favor them. Slywotzky, Morrison, and Andelman ([1997]) call this fourth fit the "profit zone," where "increased focus on the core business is likely to pay off" (p. 7). Similarly, Bain consultants Chris Zook and James Allen, in their book *Profit from the Core* (2001), assert and document that success comes from a creative search for opportunities that match up well with the firm's core business: "We have found that the key to unlocking hidden sources of growth and profits is not to abandon the core business but to focus on it with renewed vigor and a new level of creativity" (p. 3).

It is clear to us from research and our consulting experience that pursuing the *desired* fit leads to sustained competitive advantage and success.

## Applying the 4Ds

4D analysis is advanced through organized discussion, which we call *guided involvement* (this is the topic of Chapter Seven) to analyze the firm's strategic situation. It helps members remove perceptual blinders through active listening and open dialogue; it also helps them reach consensus on strategic issues. It reveals faulty assumptions and corrects for misleading conclusions. It further helps participants deal constructively with political resistance and conflicts that invariably arise when some are wedded to the status quo or have different self-interests or points of view.

We engage top management teams in strategy-making at off-site retreats that promote open dialogue and consensus building free from work and family demands. The first part of the retreat is devoted to strategic assessment. We start by presenting a summary of the SWOT information previously collected from team members through personal interviews or short e-mail surveys. We then ask if they agree with its conclusions and whether to add or subtract anything.

This sets the stage to introduce the 4D model, but without labels in each box because they might bias members to focus on only the *desired* quadrant. Our experience suggests that the 4D framework is useful for organizing SWOT data in these settings. It leads to spirited discussion and insights that might not readily happen by simply arranging information under the four categories of strengths, weaknesses, opportunities, and threats. Moreover, the framework provides on-the-spot analysis resulting in immediate findings that can be quickly shared among members using a common language. This helps them reach collective agreement on conclusions from their strategic assessment, so they can proceed expeditiously to set strategic direction, subject to further checking with middle managers and the workforce.

To use the 4D framework, we break the management team into small subgroups and ask each to begin an analysis of the company and its competitive environment by discussing alternate strategies for their firm in each of the four quadrants. The use of subgroups gives each member space and time to talk and reveals how much members agree or disagree when the subgroups later share and compare their results. They typically conclude that Boxes I, II, and III are largely reactive strategies that eat up time and money and lack long-term viability. Most appealing is Box IV. We end this assessment task by letting participants know the labels we have put on each box.

Then we ask the team, again divided into subgroups, to focus more in-depth on Box IV. Each subgroup is asked to analyze further the firm's unique capabilities and match them with specific market opportunities. We remind them that a creative search for opportunities that match up well with the firm's core business is a necessary prelude to strategic success. To guide this assessment, we give the subgroups clear instructions to focus on the firm's core products or services and key capabilities. They are asked to provide concrete answers to the following questions:

1. Is there a future in this market for growth?
2. What does the customer want from us that we aren't providing?
3. What are our competitors providing? What are their strengths and weaknesses?
4. What do we have in the way of capabilities to outwit our competitors?
5. What is the best fit between capabilities and market opportunities?
6. What features would we have to add to compete? Can we produce them? What would be their cost?

For example, the Petrofuels Energy team, in focusing attention on the *desired* quadrant, concluded that while there was a market for additional services, such as pipeline repairs and extermination with their varied customers, they didn't have the know-how or capability to diversify into these services. They concluded they knew fuel distribution a lot better. We shall see in Chapter Six that Petrofuels's managers found good opportunities for growth in their fuel market, which they previously and mistakenly believed was a mature market.

## Assessing Slack

We encourage participants to consider organizational and market slack in their analysis. Slack can provide the space to move in a new strategic direction; lack of slack is problematic.

*Organizational Slack.* Firms that have unused assets and are accustomed to change have the slack needed for strategic change. Extra resources and time enable firms to discover and take advantage of new opportunities. Experience with change also helps them overcome resistance and feel more comfortable with innovation.

Organizations with low organizational slack find it difficult, if not impossible, to change strategically or rapidly. They tend to focus on exploiting the status quo and have few resources left for exploration and invention. In these cases, strategic change is likely to require drastic interventions like replacing key leaders, restructuring the corporation, or creating a sense of urgency for change among employees (Bourgeois and Singh, 1983).

*Market Slack.* Economists have long talked about market slack as an incentive for managers to act strategically (Voss, Sirdeshmukh, and Voss, 2008). This usually occurs when there are inefficiencies in the market, such as when Petrofuels's management team discovered they were competing against lots of inefficient small mom-and-pop distributors. Slack is often hidden, waiting to be uncovered through analysis and open discussion. Some firms are competing in markets where there is little possibility to innovate or move, typically in highly regulated markets or ones where the industry price structure is inelastic and huge amounts of capital are needed to move forward. More favorable high-slack environments exist where there is fast industry growth with lots of competitive openings and the costs of movement and investment are not too high.

*Improving Slack.* Finding or creating the ideal situation, where both organizational and market slack are high, may be a daunting task, requiring a good deal of creativity, tenacity, and skillful action. Petrofuels's CEO, Wil Martin, faced seemingly low organizational *and* market slack, in that the organization was resistant and the firm's product (fuel) had to compete in a commodity market. He first took steps to increase organizational slack by motivating his team to make budget successfully before attacking strategic issues. This gave him added credibility to pursue strategic change. Martin then focused his team on the marketplace to find a higher-price niche where Petrofuels could win over customers by ensuring good delivery service and a high level of safety that mom-and-pop competitors could not provide. Petrofuels also gained slack by freeing up cash from selling off noncore assets and exiting certain markets where it had low market share.

## Analysis Requires Creativity

Our experience in applying the 4D framework suggests three potential pitfalls or challenges that can impede strategic assessment. Careful attention to them can move analysis ahead successfully.

The first challenge for most participants lies in the search for a *desired* fit. It is relatively easy to identify organizational strengths, but more difficult to locate market opportunities, and even harder to discover or create the right match between the two. Market opportunities do not stand out easily; often they are found only through extensive analysis and creativity, such as when Procter & Gamble developed the Swiffer mop instead of a new detergent. At Petrofuels, top management discussed and debated at length strategic alternatives about whether to diversify into new areas or continue to focus on its core business of fuel distribution. The final decision to stay with the core business required a lot of hard work, insight, and persistence.

The second challenge arises when an organization discovers that specific strengths useful in the past need to be revised or replaced by new capabilities. This was the case when Kodak realized very late that digital photography was replacing chemical photography (Swasy, 1997). Any turnaround to build new capabilities can come at a high cost, and firms need to recognize and take potential costs into account in making their strategic assessment. Otherwise they can easily fall into a downward spiral, with one bad strategic choice leading to another, as Sheth documents in *The Self-Destructive Habits of Good Companies: And How to Break Them* (2007).

The third challenge is that industries vary in economic structure and the organizational forms and practices that can succeed in them (Rumelt, 1991). Their 4D analysis must be sensitive to these differences, especially when considering how the organization's capabilities fit external opportunities. Consider the economic contrast between the oil and the entertainment industries, for example. Firms in the oil industry can do very little in real time to find oil because massive amounts of capital have to be poured into oil exploration and drilling, with the payout uncertain and years off. The entertainment industry invests millions in films that can succeed or fail over three opening weekends, a real-time outcome. Both industries pose high degrees of risk, but with different time frames and rates of change. Or consider the organizational differences in the automobile industry. American firms are notorious for their resistance to change, while Japanese competitors are particularly good at continuous improvement and innovation, notably at Toyota and Honda with their hybrids. Attention to these economic and organizational differences helps to ensure that assessment data are interpreted and understood within their industry context.

## From Abstract Conclusions to Written Statements

Assessments by management are in abstract form; they have to be made more concrete for action taking. In the next chapter, we take up the main vehicle for doing so, the statement of strategic direction, which is written and organized around elements in the implementing format. The statement translates abstract thinking into a more concrete and understandable form, which can then offer an effective communication tool to check for validity and agreement, as well as to communicate with and inspire the workforce.

# 6

# CRAFTING A STRATEGIC STATEMENT

When executives complete their strategic assessment and discover a promising market opportunity that closely matches the firm's capabilities, what they have is a mere abstraction of a future strategy as an analytical conclusion in their heads. This abstraction requires concrete form to become visible. Needed is a straightforward framework to define, record, and implement a new strategy—a clear, understandable, and action-oriented format that turns strategy into reality. For us and our clients, this abstract strategy takes on life by preparing and writing a clear statement of strategic direction.

## Value of Written Statement and Organized Format

Little guidance exists in the strategy literature as to the need for writing out the strategy or the appropriate format to organize the strategic content. Companies use different approaches to create and convey their strategies. Some write long reports that are obsessively detailed, some talk rather than write, and some simply list bullet points under this commonly recommended format by McKinsey consultants: "issues, objectives, and action steps" (Dye and Sibony, 2007).

In terms of level of abstraction, many statements of strategy result in words that seem to come from thirty thousand feet, leaving organization members "on the ground" to impute their own interpretations, misinterpretations, and general misunderstandings. For example, consider this vision and values statement published by a financial institution:

> Our company will continue to endeavor to be a provider of financial services and products that customers need and want. The company will maintain strategic and organizational flexibility to meet the challenges with the dynamics of the changing industry landscape. In pursuing its vision, the company will endeavor to maintain an environment which encourages employee integrity, creativity, a spirit of excitement and personal growth; rewards high performance and ensures a high level of customer satisfaction [Abrahams, 2007, p. 102].

Some appear as mission statements that describe only what the institution does, not its future direction. Others appear as vision and values statements for what the firm will ideally look like in five or ten years. These have been widely criticized for their lack of strategic substance (notably economics, marketing, and organization) and failure to be implemented. Promising a vision that can't be delivered will likely lead to widespread cynicism among organization members (Ready and Conger, 2008). Reality trumps hope.

## Written Statement of Strategic Direction

The idea of a statement of strategic direction is not new; for example, Johnson & Johnson, the high-performing health care giant, has been guided by one for many years, although it is written in prose and with a different structure from our own format (see Appendix D for the J&J statement).

In *dynamic strategy-making*, a written strategic statement serves two purposes with regard to content: (1) provides a way to ascertain agreement among those who formed it, as well as a basis to communicate the new strategy later, and (2) gives the structure and anatomy of what will become the foundation of a new strategic system. First, we explain the purpose and the value of placing the statement in writing. Then we discuss the all-important format with examples from two cases, Petrofuels Energy and Near-Ritz, a hotel chain that was a recent client for us.

We believe that every strategy should be put in writing to reduce room for future misinterpretation by indicating a clear path ahead. We call this a *statement of strategic direction*. It is not a mission statement or vision and values statement because the former describes what the firm does today and the latter records the abstract aspirations of managers. Both are neither comprehensive nor sensitive to market structures and economics.

The statement is a concrete product and a sign of accomplishment that pulls and drives the top team through the strategy-making process. Brevity adds clarity. Bain consultants Gadiesh and Gilbert (2001) contend that such statements prove invaluable when composed as follows: "The distillation of a company's strategy into a pithy, memorable, and prescriptive phrase is important because a brilliant business strategy, like an insightful approach to warfare, is of little use unless people understand it well enough to apply it—both to anticipated decisions and unforeseen opportunities" (p. 3). The statement has to be written, quickly prepared, and readily renewed when events change. It should be stated in words that are specific and easy for all employees to understand and implement. Early in the process, it provides a way to test and validate a draft for its realism and achievability. Later it provides a way to communicate and inspire the workforce, as well as to inform other stakeholders, like investors.

We prefer that the statement be kept simple (though not overly simple) with the content stated on one page in bullet points, which makes it easy to review and use as talking points in articulating the strategy to the workforce and others. It makes strategic content more operational and lively. These statements, and excerpts from them, can also be used to measure progress and screen investments and organization changes, provide talking points with employees, support presentations for the board and outside investors, create advertising messages, and serve as public relations messages.

## Four Key Elements

The statement of strategic direction is constructed and written around what we call *four key elements* that form the skeleton of a strategic system, thereby allowing the meat of strategic content to be placed on it and revised over time. The format also guides executives' strategic thinking and dialogue to realistic conclusions about strategic direction. There are four essential elements (see Figure 6.1):

- *Competitive logic.* The growth engine from 4D assessment (market position and customer tiebreakers), describing how the firm will compete into the future

### Figure 6.1 The Four Elements

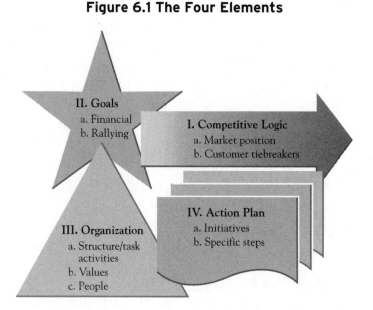

- *Goals.* The unifying target for achievement, separated into financial goals and a single rallying goal
- *Organization.* The means for strategic content to be embedded into the structure, shared values (culture), and people
- *Action plan.* The initiatives and specific steps, which lay out a path to implement the strategic system that will ensure everyone behaves the strategy in their daily behavior

The content placed on the four elements is the essence of the strategy that comprises the backbone of a new strategic system, thereby charting an organization's direction forward. We listed them above in the order in which they are addressed in the off-site retreats described in Chapter Seven. The group begins with *competitive logic,* which derives from conclusions reached in the 4D analysis about fitting the firm's capabilities to the environment's opportunities. Then the other three elements—goals, organization, and action plan—are aligned closely with the competitive logic so as to support its implementation. They spell out exactly what is to be achieved, how the organization will be structured to accomplish it, and what steps are needed to make this happen. The combined effect is to position the firm in the market and tightly link its objectives, structure, and actions to that strategy.

We arrived at the four elements after experimenting with several alternatives in various projects and reviewing available descriptions of strategy-making in the literature. We culled and synthesized from a large list of potential strategy content those elements that we believe are absolutely essential for creating strategy and turning it into reality. For example, we considered such important and commonly advocated dimensions as compensation and information systems, but rejected them because they seem to flow naturally once the four essential elements are in place.

In our experience, the four elements are straightforward and easy for organization members to understand and remember.

And memory is important in a real-time world that frequently requires spontaneous responses without having to stop and analyze. Like improvisation in jazz where there is melody to hold things together as musicians invent around it, the four essential elements provide an operational format around which organizations can constantly update and reinvent strategic content as real-time circumstances demand.

The examples from client statements in Exhibits 6.1 through 6.4 illustrate and explain the content of each element; these come from real-time strategy-making by Petrofuels, a distributor of many types of fuel across the country, and the Near-Ritz hotel chain that operates across the southern United States and is led by CEO Alice Smith. Their statements of strategic direction are shown in Exhibits 6.1 and 6.2, respectively. (All of the exhibits are at the end of the chapter.) We have included two additional statement examples from other clients: Exhibit 6.3 for an energy company and Exhibit 6.4, a prose version for a child care organization that was written for communication to thousands in its workforce. Each statement was created by the top leadership team in a series of structured off-site retreats, aided by a facilitator who helped to speed up decision making in a real-time mode.

## Element I: Determine Competitive Logic

An effective strategy should center on a value proposition that connects the firm's strengths to unique market opportunities. It serves as the firm's growth engine and ties it to the marketplace leading to greater growth and better performance. We call this proposition the *competitive logic*, which includes both *market position*, and another often overlooked element, *customer tiebreakers*, which represent the hard-to-discover features that attract and retain customers. The competitive logic is derived from the 4D analysis and comes first because it is the brain of strategic content and cues the formulation of the other three essential elements.

For example, Accenture Consulting has a competitive logic that focuses on the many services that go with information system design and operations for large global clients with big projects for substantial but reasonable fees. Accenture's tiebreakers include worldwide delivery of consulting services through its many global offices, leading-edge knowledge to stay on the forefront, and a highly trained and home-grown workforce, most of whom leave Accenture within ten years for good positions and eventually become clients.

## Identify Market Position

This part of competitive logic describes how products and services should be positioned and priced in the market relative to competitors. The 4D analysis and assessment helps executives to create market position by identifying an opportunity where a firm can compete effectively and grow, using its core capabilities and resources. As we have pointed out, it is not easy for members to identify a logic that will be successful. It is not a static proposition about how to relate to the market today but is the growth engine that should last for a few years and be revised when competitive conditions call for it.

### Petrofuels Example

> Focus exclusively on marketing and distributing fuels (propane and aircraft) and achieve rapid growth through:
>
> - Modest increase in prices (average two cents per gallon) in return for special features to customer
> - Set aggressive financial goals
> - Make acquisitions
> - Exit low-share markets
> - Sell-off nonpetrofuel assets for cash

Petrofuels's management team created a competitive logic where it chose to remain in and focus on the petrofuel business rather than diversify into other services like tank and pipeline repair. In addition, the logic called for aggressive financial goals; more selectivity in choosing its geographical markets; pricing its product higher than competition in return for customer tiebreakers of added safety and service; and growing through the acquisition of smaller, inefficient competitors. Previously Petrofuels pursued a very different competitive logic that led from weakness, diversifying defensively out of petrofuel into unrelated products, not being selective in choosing its geographical markets with growth potential, settling for low cash flow goals to satisfy its parents, and failing to consider acquisitions.

## Near-Ritz Example

Build brand and expand throughout the South as a four-star chain.

- Through management contracts and acquisitions when contracts not available
- Priced just under five-star hotels
- Target the conference and group meeting segments

The management of Near-Ritz, a four-star hotel chain based in the South, decided to limit its competitive logic to future growth in the southern United States because it had little international experience. Another option would have been to go national or international through acquisitions, which promised good growth; moreover, Near-Ritz had the financial resources and the opportunity to do a deal. This alternative growth path was tempting, but it required additional costs associated with developing new know-how and other capabilities to become a competitive player. So senior management decided to focus on market opportunities where it already had strengths with brand recognition in the sun belt region, ranging from Florida to Arizona, where Near-Ritz could price itself just under better-known five-star hotels while targeting conferences and business travelers.

It also chose a low-capital way to grow by pursuing management contracts of existing hotels or from real estate developers wanting to build hotels and left room to acquire some hotels and remodel them when management contracts were not available.

## Create Customer Tiebreakers

The competitive logic is not complete unless it identifies those precise features we call *customer tiebreakers* to attract and retain customers. Strategy is about being unique and attractive in the eyes of customers, and tiebreakers make the firm's products and services stand out relative to what competitors offer. Most competitors have similar strengths residing in good products, up-to-date technology, and hard-working employees. So the challenge becomes one of identifying the unique and differentiating features that build off existing strengths to attract new customers and lure buyers away from competitors.

Two key questions help to determine tiebreakers: What three to four features from the customer's point of view are likely to determine his or her purchases in the future? And which of these features best fit our competencies to perform and deliver them? Usually more than one tiebreaker is required, and rarely are they based solely on price. Instead, more subtle features that exist in various combinations of cost, quality, and service are essential to create attractive features. For example, there is the UPS brown truck image of reliable service and delivery, Procter & Gamble's marketing and brand management system, Johnson & Johnson's credo and its reputation for being ethical and trustworthy, and the McDonald's emphasis on cleanliness and consistent quality worldwide.

### Petrofuels Example

- Exceptional standards of safety
- High standards of delivery—"service before you need us"
- Emphasize marketing

Petrofuels emphasized new customer tiebreakers of enhanced marketing, with increased safety, and "service before you need us" to attract customers willing to pay a small premium for these features. Management recognized that the product was an undifferentiated commodity and therefore price sensitive, but it is also dangerous, so safety is clearly important to customers who depend on it for travel, distribution, heating, and cooking. Many Petrofuels competitors were small mom-and-pop distributors that did not provide this level of service with on-time delivery and assurances of safety. So Petrofuels management bet that customers would be willing to pay an average of two cents more per gallon of petrofuel for these features. And they were right. The marginal revenue from this premium went directly to Petrofuels's bottom line.

### Near-Ritz Example

- Informal and friendly atmosphere
- Good food at reasonable prices
- Ease of business services
- A superb conference experience

Near-Ritz identified these tiebreakers because conference and group business were large profit makers, and five-star locations were too expensive. In this way, the chain sought to build its regional brand image by attracting business customers and conferences. Management assumed that business customers who had a good meeting experience would return in the future as individual customers.

Many organizations stop at this point, believing that their strategy is complete, or they will jump directly to an action plan. But if the competitive logic is to take on a life and make a difference, it must be translated into goals, organization, and action plans. Without these changes, the old strategy is likely to remain in practice.

## Element II: Set Key Goals

Two kinds of goals are essential: *financial goals* that will direct effort and measure progress and a single *rallying goal* that will motivate the workforce to embrace the strategy, especially for those who may not be excited by abstract financial goals. Specific and clear goals help to unify and motivate employees to make the strategy happen.

Once goals are accomplished, new ones can be set and added to the statement. Collins and Porras (1996), in talking about their experience with Big Hairy Audacious Goals (BHAG), state: "People like to shoot for finish lines" (p. 72). Recent research suggests that when top management teams agree on a few financial goals and their importance, their firm's performance is higher than it would have been otherwise (Colbert, Kirstof-Brown, Bradley, and Barrick, 2008). Regrettably, lots of organizations set too many performance goals and wind up diluting energy and diverting focus from strategic accomplishment.

### Decide Financial Goals

Challenging financial goals must be logically and tightly linked to the competitive logic. To be effective, they must be understandable, easily measured and communicated, and tied to compensation. They should also be a stretch, quantified with a time frame, like "increase sales by 15 percent a year over the next two years." In addition to directing and motivating employee behavior, financial goals can help to screen future investment decisions to ensure they are consistent with the competitive logic.

#### Petrofuels Example

- "Double sales and profits in five years."

Previously, Petrofuels's only financial goal was to generate cash to pay off short-term interest on its parent's leveraged buyout debt. However, this new financial goal established a higher standard, requiring it to drive growth from both sales and acquisitions. It accomplished this goal in less than three years.

### Near-Ritz Example

- "Each hotel should achieve 30 percent net operating profit within two years."

Near-Ritz's management set a challenging but realistic financial goal of achieving 30 percent net operating profit within two years for all forty hotels. Previously hotels were not treated as profit centers. This new goal shifted responsibility and accountability to each hotel and its general manager for results. Within two years, all hotels were at or above 30 percent net operating profit.

## Create Rallying Goal

The rallying goal, which is often overlooked as a legitimate goal, can motivate the wider workforce to pursue the strategic direction, since many employees may not identify with abstract financial goals. The rallying goal provides a collective purpose for the workforce, helping to reinforce the strategy. Successful strategy implementation relies on frontline employees' committing to where the firm is headed, and behaving its tiebreakers in their daily actions.

### Petrofuels Example

- "Double in 5"

Petrofuels's rallying goal became "Double in 5," which is similar to its financial goal but stated without explicit reference to sales and profits. This rallying goal gave new hope to employees. It suggested that the company was indeed on the move, which would increase career opportunities and wages.

## *Near-Ritz Example*

- "Best Service in the South for Groups and Conferences"

This rallying goal for the hotel chain was closely aligned with its competitive logic of expansion throughout the South, targeting the conference segment, and its tiebreaker of providing better service to business customers.

## Element III: Align Organization

This essential element involves the design of a formal organization structure that aligns people with tasks to promote fit with its competitive logic and goals; without them, the strategy might easily remain a plaque on the wall. Most important is to make organization changes that will realize the competitive logic. This can be structural changes like placing the right people in the right jobs, such as Near-Ritz converting its hotels into profit centers led by strong leaders acting as general managers. It may also involve a new set of values to reflect the tiebreakers, such as Petrofuels's "service before you need us." Strategic leaders should clarify, communicate, and model new values in their behavior for others to emulate and follow.

Another challenge is to build a high-performance organization that is both agile and flexible, enabling it to change rapidly in a real-time world. Today many traditional firms undergoing strategic change may have to transform almost their entire organization to align with the new strategy and direct the workforce to move in a new strategic direction. The following unique characteristics of these new organizations are geared to achieving high performance in a 24/7 world (Galbraith, Downey, and Kates, 2002; Lawler and Worley, 2006):

- *Flat, lean organization structures* to break down functional silos and push decision making downward in the organization,

so employees can respond flexibly and rapidly to changing
conditions

- *Work designs*, such as self-managed teams, to support
employees with high levels of discretion, task variety, and
meaningful feedback to encourage employee responsibility
and teamwork

- *Open information systems* to provide necessary and timely
information for employees to participate meaningfully in
goal setting and decision making

- *Human resource practices* to ensure that people with the
right expertise and values are selected, developed, and provided with significant career opportunities

- *Reward systems*, based on performance and skill development, to motivate and reinforce organization learning and
performance

## Design Organization Structure and Task Activities

There are many possible organization structures for management
to consider, ranging from functional to product configurations,
centralized or decentralized. The challenge is to design only
important and necessary changes consistent with the logic and
goals. Too much change takes eyes off the strategy. For example,
if a new marketing department is required to focus on tiebreakers,
that may be all that is necessary. According to Nadler and
Tushman (1997), these are the key questions to ask in choosing
an organization structure:

- What should be the basic units of structure?
- What is each unit accountable for?
- How should the units relate to each other? What coordi-
nating mechanisms are needed?
- What is the role of corporate staff? How should it be struc-
tured?

- What should be the major policymaking and decision-making committees?

The effective grouping of task activities into clusters along the value chain is highlighted by Porter (1996) as an important differentiating factor. Each change requires some rearranging to fit people with tasks.

### Petrofuels Example

- New aggressive marketing department
- Rename and reorient old marketing department to become operations
- Add acquisitions team reporting to CEO
- Combine supply and transportation to get better service
- Reduce twenty-four division managers to fourteen best managers
- Eliminate zone managers to get top management closer to field
- Put all staff under one senior vice president who reports to CEO
- New executive committee of five senior vice presidents and CEO

Petrofuels made several organizational changes to reinforce its new competitive logic, tiebreakers, and financial goals. It established a customer-facing marketing department to replace a reactive practice of relying on orders over the phone. A new acquisitions department was added to identify and pursue likely targets. To get better service for customers, the supply and transportation departments were combined into a task cluster. Organization levels were flattened in the field organization, where zones and divisions were reduced and streamlined. All corporate staff departments, including human resources, information technology, legal, and accounting, were placed under a single manager reporting to the CEO to ensure that the value of service was practiced internally. The executive committee was restructured and made smaller to make it more efficient.

## Near-Ritz Example

- Decentralize with each hotel serving as a profit center
- Add marketing of conferences at headquarters and in each hotel
- Add corporate development department reporting to CEO to pursue management contracts and make acquisitions of small chains when feasible

The firm moved away from tight headquarters control to decentralize its hotels into decentralized profit centers, which aligned them with the new financial goal of 30 percent net operating profit for each hotel. It also set up a headquarters staff group to solicit national conferences, as well as adding a marketing person in each hotel to promote meetings of business groups. Previously each hotel's organization structure was split into separate functions reporting straight upward to centralized control at headquarters; the role of general manager was relegated to act as a public relations person in the community. The new structure of decentralized hotels as profit centers was intended to empower each hotel and its general manager to run its own show. Additional help was added at headquarters to develop management contracts with real estate developers, and to make acquisitions of small chains.

## Create Shared Values

Values are deep-seated beliefs that become norms. In organizations, they tell members what is important, what to pay attention to, and how to behave. *Shared values* become part of the organizational culture; they tie members to the strategy and to each other. Shared values along with leadership are the glue that holds the workforce together (Schein, 2004). They are especially needed in today's organizations that operate around the world, where employees are often out of sight of their supervisors and fellow coworkers. Values also guide and reinforce key behaviors so they are consistent with the customer tiebreakers. For example, a value like teamwork might direct members to "let customers know we are a team and behave it." After all, if they don't behave the values toward each other, how will they behave it toward customers?

### Petrofuels Example

- Unified teamwork
- Aggressive marketing
- High standards of safety
- High standards of service ("Service before you need us")

Petrofuels opted for values centered on teamwork, service, and safety—all intended to reinforce tiebreakers for customers. Training and recognition programs were created to educate and reward behaviors consistent with these new values. Managers received favorable performance appraisals for reinforcing these values through their leadership behavior.

### Near-Ritz Example

- If a customer complains and it's our fault, comp their room
- Every hotel is a team
- Details count at conferences
- Be informal and friendly

The hotel chain adopted new values related to customer satisfaction, teamwork, and attention to details. These values were aligned with the new tiebreakers and the rallying goal of emphasizing service to attract profitable conferences.

## Assign People

No strategy moves forward without having the right people in the right positions. Depending on the magnitude of organization change required to enact the new strategy, firms may simply reassign members to new positions or may need to hire people with entirely new skill sets and expertise. In our experience, assigning people to the right positions requires clarification of the skills needed in each job to enact the strategy, as well as making a careful assessment of whether existing members or newcomers have or can rapidly acquire them. Because skills are likely to have a short shelf life in today's rapidly changing environments, organizations need to plan for constant training and development of the workforce. Too often training is not connected to the strategy of the firm (Boudreau and Ramstad, 2007).

### Petrofuels Example

- All 5 top managers changed positions to match their qualifications
- Thirty-four other managers switched positions
- Acquisitions expert hired reporting to CEO
- New senior vice president appointed to oversee all staff and reporting to CEO
- Profit sharing introduced for all employees

At Petrofuels, thirty-nine managers, including five senior vice presidents, switched jobs in the company to get the right person in the right job. With all these appointments, fresh ideas were brought to each job, and new energy was released. A fifth new senior vice president was appointed to oversee all the firm's staff functions. An acquisitions department reporting to the CEO was created with new people who knew how to do acquisitions.

### Near-Ritz Example

- Put general manager in charge of each hotel
- Add conference marketing person to each hotel and at headquarters
- Add corporate development department reporting to CEO to pursue contracts and acquire small chains

The role of the hotel GM was changed from its former public relations emphasis to assume complete accountability for hotel performance, with a good incentive bonus for making progress toward 30 percent operating profit. A conference marketing coordinator was assigned to each hotel. A new finance person was hired at headquarters to search out and arrange management contracts with individual hotels and to acquire smaller chains across the South.

## Element IV: Establish Action Plan

The *action plan* lays out how the organization will go about implementing the new strategy. It sets priorities and spells out what things need to happen over what time frame to move forward. Action plans are generally organized around four to six broad initiatives that take their cue and substance directly from the content on the other three elements. Too many initiatives divert energy, make accountability vague, and cause employees to lose focus.

Each initiative usually requires three or four specific steps to cause implementation. These steps should specify responsibilities, accountabilities, and deadlines, and should be evaluated realistically for costs, benefits, and feasibility in moving the competitive logic ahead. The action plan is continuously revised when initiatives are accomplished and when real-time events make changes necessary.

### Petrofuels Example

- *Initiative 1*: Emphasize marketing, safety and service through training, painting trucks and adding new ones, and installing incentives for the sales force. Explain to current customers what they will receive in special services for slightly increased prices. Exit markets with low potential.
- *Initiative 2*: Make organizational changes, combining supply and transportation for more efficient service; reorganize departments;

streamline the field organization by reducing levels and regions; and install profit-sharing plan.

- *Initiative 3*: Communicate new strategic direction and growth plans by holding celebration at headquarters to announce changes and rallying goal. CEO goes to the field to talk up strategy and tiebreakers with the workforce. Establish a strategy review group to monitor progress.

- *Initiative 4*: Create a corporate development group reporting to CEO. Hire an acquisitions expert who knows the industry and act to sell off nonfuels assets.

Petrofuels's action plan was intended to persuade customers to pay an average of two cents more per gallon than prices charged by less reliable competitors. Its first initiative emphasized advertising and calling customers about the price increase and explaining what the customer would receive for it. A second initiative concerned making organization changes that included a new marketing department, combining the supply department with transportation to improve delivery service, placing all corporate staff functions under one person, eliminating a level in the field hierarchy, and installing a profit-sharing plan. The third initiative had to do with communicating the strategic statement to the workforce; a fourth involved selling off unrelated assets to generate cash to pay for acquisitions. At the end of one year, the company had greatly exceeded its profit plan, made five acquisitions, and its return on assets was up 40 percent.

### Near-Ritz Example

- *Initiative 1*: Identify the best people for the general manager job in each hotel; make them profit centers to get to the new financial goal of 30 percent operating profit within two years for all hotels.

- *Initiative 2*: Go after the conference business. Appoint marketing person at headquarters and in each hotel. Close down high-end restaurants in some hotels because they don't fit with the tiebreaker of "reasonable prices."

- *Initiative 3*: Win new management contracts at hotels throughout the South. Appoint an experienced manager to implement. Also make acquisitions when contracts not available.

- *Initiative 4*: Communicate new strategy to the workforce at celebration conferences. Get hotel general managers to report on what they have done to implement new strategy in their hotels. Set up ongoing strategy review group.

Near-Ritz's action plan was to implement the logic of focusing and expanding in the South with its four-star chain. One initiative was to select the best managers for general manager positions in each hotel who would have complete responsibility as a profit center. Another step was to strengthen its marketing efforts to attract conferences and corporate meetings because they were high-profit items. Here they added marketing directors in each hotel as well as to the staff at headquarters. They also began an initiative to pursue management contracts at hotels, as well as make acquisitions of small hotel chains. Finally, they set up a process of communicating the strategy to each hotel, setting up groups in each hotel to follow up on implementation.

## Next Chapter: From Statement (Content) to Guided Involvement (Process)

The strategic content of the statements was created through a process we call guided involvement, the subject of the next chapter. It is an organized process of discussion and discovery within the management team. This is no easy task; real-time strategic content doesn't arrive on a silver platter from ad hoc meetings or from short visioning sessions, or from time-consuming studies. It requires skillful leadership and expert facilitation, the subjects of Chapters Eight and Nine. This involvement process is used to inspire and guide middle management and the workforce to embrace, follow, and revise the new strategic direction embedded in the strategic system.

## Exhibit 6.1 Petrofuels Energy: Statement of Strategic Direction

I. Determine Competitive Logic
   a. Identify market position: Focus exclusively on marketing and distributing fuels (propane to aircraft) and achieve rapid growth through:
      - Modest increase in prices (average two cents per gallon) in return for special features to customer
      - Set aggressive financial goals
      - Make acquisitions
      - Exit low-share markets
      - Sell off nonpetrofuel assets
   b. Create customer tiebreakers:
      - Exceptional standards of safety
      - High standards of delivery—"service before you need us"
      - Emphasize marketing

II. Set Goals
   a. Decide financial goal:
      - "Double Sales and Profits in Five Years"
   b. Create rallying goal:
      - "Double in 5"

III. Align Organization
   a. Design organization structure and task activities:
      - New aggressive marketing department
      - Rename and reorient old Marketing to become Operations
      - Add acquisitions team reporting to CEO
      - Combine supply and transportation to get better service
      - Reduce twenty-four division managers to fourteen best managers
      - Eliminate zone managers to get top management closer to field
      - Put all staff under one senior vice president report to CEO
      - New executive committee of five senior vice presidents and CEO
   b. Create shared values:
      - Unified teamwork
      - Aggressive marketing

- High standards of safety
- High standards of service

c. Assign people:

- All 5 top managers change positions to match their qualifications
- Thirty-four other managers switch positions
- Acquisitions expert hired
- New senior vice president appointed to oversee all staff and reporting to CEO
- Install profit-sharing plan for all employees

IV. Launch Action Plan

*Initiative 1*: Place emphasis on marketing safety and service

*Specific steps*

- Create marketing department; advertise to customers
- Initiate service training for truck drivers
- Paint old trucks and buy new ones
- Sales incentives for sales force
- Identify and exit markets with low potential
- Explain to current customers what they will receive for slightly increased prices

*Initiative 2*: Make organization changes

*Specific steps*

- Combine supply and transportation departments
- Reduce levels and regions in field organization
- Establish senior vice president over all staff functions

*Initiative 3*: Communicate new strategic direction and growth plans

*Specific steps*

- Hold celebration at headquarters to announce changes and rallying goal
- CEO meetings to talk up strategy and tiebreakers with workforce in the field
- Set up strategy review committee

*Initiative 4*: Create corporate development group reporting to CEO

*Specific steps*

- Hire acquisitions expert
- Senior vice presidents suggest potential targets to group
- Sell off nonpetrofuel assets for cash

## Exhibit 6.2 Near-Ritz Hotel Chain: Statement of Strategic Direction

I. Determine Competitive Logic

  a. Identify market position
- "Build brand and expand throughout the South as a four-star chain"
- Through management contracts and acquisitions when contracts not available
- Priced just under five-star hotels
- Target the conference and group meeting segments

  b. Create customer tiebreakers
- Informal and friendly atmosphere
- Good food at reasonable prices
- Ease of business services
- A superb conference experience

II. Set Key Goals

  a. Decide financial goal
- Each hotel should achieve 30 percent operating profit within two years.

  b. Create rallying goal
- "Best Service in the South for Groups and Conferences"

III. Align Organization

  a. Design organization structure and task activities
- Decentralize with each hotel serving as a profit center
- Add marketing of conferences at headquarters and in each hotel
- Add corporate development department reporting to CEO to pursue management contracts and make acquisitions of small chains when feasible

  b. Create shared values
- If a customer complains and it's our fault, comp their room
- Every hotel is a team
- Details count at conferences
- Be informal and friendly

    c. Assign people

- Put general manager in charge of each hotel
- Add conference marketing person to each hotel and at headquarters

IV. Launch Action Plan (Initiatives and Specific Steps Combined)

*Initiative 1*: Identify best people for general manager job in each hotel; make them profit centers to get to new goals of 30 percent operating profit.

*Initiative 2*: Go after the conference business. Appoint marketing person at headquarters in each hotel. Close down high-end restaurants in some hotels because they don't fit with the tiebreaker of "reasonable prices."

*Initiative 3*: Win new management contracts at hotels throughout the South. Appoint an experienced manager to implement. Also make acquisitions when contracts not available.

*Initiative 4*: Communicate new strategy to the workforce at celebration conferences. Get hotel general managers to report on what they have done to implement new strategy in their hotels. Set up ongoing strategy review group.

**Exhibit 6.3 XYZ Energy: Statement of Strategic Direction**

I. Determine Competitive Logic

Identify market position

- Cost-conscious customers looking for high-quality gas (five cents per gallon lower)
- Self-service stations located in only five southeastern states
- Cash purchases only
- All crude provided by company-owned Indonesian reserves
- Two highly efficient refineries in Texas and New Jersey
- Provide high-margin impulse soft drinks and snack foods

Create tiebreakers

- No-hassle purchase: clean, efficient, safe service stations
- Located within easy driving from home and on way to work
- Strong customer orientation; act friendly and courteous at all times
- Can easily purchase snacks and drinks for consumption in car

II. Set Goals

Decide financial goal

- Increase market share from 20 percent to 24 percent within three years
- Reduce operating costs by $100 million within three years

Create rallying goal

- #1 in South
- One hundred new stations in two years

III. Align Organization

Design organization structure and task activities

- Each station is a profit center with positive cash flow
- Lean corporate staff focused on serving operations
- Incentive pay for achievement of financial goals

Create shared values and assign people

- Be environmentally conscious in all operations

- Do not sacrifice quality or safety for earnings
- Be good corporate citizen; support communities where we live

IV. Launch Action Plan

*Initiative 1*: Replace all single-product pumps with high-speed multiple-product-dispensing pumps by end of year

*Specific steps*

1. Set up task force to move project forward—complete in six months

2. Allocate $2 million to project

*Initiative 2*: Hire new advertising firm to enhance quality/price image for APC (advanced petroleum content) gasoline

*Specific steps*

1. Select firm in six weeks, launch in three months

2. Appoint R. W. Smith to manage the project

*Initiative 3*: Institute new incentive pay plan to focus on cost reductions

*Specific steps*

1. Reduce costs by 15 percent over the next year

2. Hire consulting firm to design new pay plan and incentives

## Exhibit 6.4 Childcare Corporation: Prose Statement of Strategic Direction

*When a new CEO entered Childcare Corporation, a leading provider of early childhood education, under a leverage buyout, he initiated a strategic effort. Childcare operated over nine hundred centers in local communities across the United States and in Europe. The CEO wanted a strategic effort to unify the company practices because he felt each center was its own independent operator. An undisciplined center (as well as the company) was vulnerable to lawsuits due to caring for children. He was also concerned about improving the overall financial performance despite customer resistance to raising rates.*

*Many high-growth markets were not being served by Childcare, and some centers were located in declining markets where occupancy rates were low. So in three off-site retreats, the senior management set a new strategic system into motion, which they converted to prose form for wider distribution in the company. The new CEO visited many regional meetings of directors to discuss the statement and what their views were on what should be done to advance it.*

*Childcare met all financial targets by the end of three years, and the firm was sold after five years for a 300 percent return to the original investors.*

## Childcare Corporation Statement of Strategic Direction

Children are our #1 priority. Each child and each parent is a cherished customer, and we treat them with warmth, sensitivity and respect. Parents have high expectations, and we always strive to exceed them. Children love coming to Childcare. Parents trust us for the exceptional care we give. They choose us over the competition because our centers are conveniently located and deliver a complete set of services that emphasize:

- An outstanding curriculum based on "whole child" development
- Safe and clean environment where children are loved and have fun
- Dedicated, well-trained and caring staff
- Operating standards that exceed states, national and industry practice
- Continuous communication with parents

Our daily decision-making is guided by a common set of values and standards that are shared by all employees:

- Commitment to excellence in everything we do
- Respect for each other, and for parents and children
- Superior customer service from all employees
- Teamwork, and open constructive communication

We are dedicated to the future growth and success of Childcare, which we will accomplish through adding new centers and improving year-on-year performance at each center. We will meet or exceed four key financial goals over the next three years:

- Increase company-wide occupancy to 72%
- Improve company-wide DOI [direct operating income] two percentage points
- Add 180 new centers
- Grow net income 30% per year

Our success depends on the actions of each employee every day at work, and we value their individual and team contributions. We celebrate our accomplishments, and we strongly support the personal growth and career development of all employees.

# 7

# USING GUIDED INVOLVEMENT

In Chapter Six, we looked at the placing of strategic content on a framework that will later serve as the skeleton of a new strategic system. Now we shift to strategic process—the activities and methods through which strategic content is created, executed, and updated. The process must be real time. Strategic process identifies the key stakeholders who should be involved in strategy-making and organizes them for meaningful interaction and decision making. Guided involvement includes stakeholders from the outset in strategy-making when the strategy is being formulated, not later during implementation, which is the frequent practice of many approaches. Senior executives must use their own experience, expertise, and judgment to create and execute a unique strategy for their firm.

Guided involvement is the central process of *dynamic strategy-making* for developing strategy and creating a strategic system. Its objective is to improve the quality of interaction and the final result. It provides an organized context that takes a comprehensive viewpoint toward strategic content: economics, markets, organization, and customers. It allows participants to use their knowledge and egos to create content and reach consensus on a strategy. In a real-time way, guided involvement speeds up strategic decisions and execution; it quickly taps information shared by those involved in strategy-making to create and record the content on the statement of strategic direction.

In *dynamic strategy-making*, guided involvement comes in two forms: (1) the structure and conduct of off-site retreats to create the strategy and strategic system, as well as other organized follow-up contexts, such as celebrations and strategy review committees, all of which provide the context for (2) social dialogue through interventions that allow the participants to advance the process constructively.

## Involvement Comes in Many Forms

Managers, consultants, and scholars have advocated many different approaches to the value of involvement for developing strategy (Cope, 1989), change (Bunker and Alban, 1978), and for use of groups to enhance involvement (Devane and Holman, 2006). It seems essential to creating and implementing strategy successfully. Failed strategies often result from lack of involvement, according to Mintzberg, Ahlstrand, and Lampel (2005):

> This is the age of the computer; the system will do it. Or will it? I believe that hard data seriously distorts any strategy-making process that relies on it.... No need to go out and meet the troops, or the customers, to find out how the products are being bought or the war is being fought. That just wastes valuable time.... Study after study has demonstrated that managers of every sort rely primarily on oral forms of communications, on the order of about 80 percent of their time [p. 114].

Although involvement can improve strategy-making, it is not a panacea when used by itself without substance or performed as a participative tool to manipulate people into accepting a foregone decision. For example, some managers claim to use participative meetings to discuss strategy, but these meetings amount to dog-and-pony slide presentations followed by superficial discussion. Strategy consultants commonly perform a strategy study from hard data supplemented by single interviews with a select sample of managers, only to be surprised later to find resistance from those left out of the sample. Some firms believe they can find the strategic answer in market research and other public data without involving key stakeholders. And many organizations just make up strategy as they go, so strategy emerges gradually out of self-interest and political compromise. These approaches of the past, many of which continue to be used, result in delays from resistance, second-guessing, and endless politics. None of that is in keeping with effective real-time strategy-making.

## Deliberate Versus Incremental Approaches

The many approaches to involvement in strategy-making generally conform to one or the other of two perspectives: a formal deliberate model and an informal incremental one. Both specify different involvement paths in strategy-making, leading to contrasting results, each with benefits and costs.

*The Formal Deliberate Model.* This conventional, *deliberate school* of strategy-making focuses mostly on content and is represented well in the strategic-planning literature (Ansoff, 1965; Vancil, 1977). It prescribes a set of formal, rational steps to strategy-making, usually carried out by experts, consultants, or senior staff, and then handed over later to senior executives for approval and implementation. Member involvement is very limited and operates from the top down, with senior managers telling others what to do. It has these typical steps:

1. Analyze the current environment.
2. Propose strategic alternatives.
3. Consider company strengths and weaknesses.
4. Determine firm strategy.
5. Align organization structure, rewards, and personnel to fit strategy.
6. Communicate strategy and organization to employees.
7. Measure results.
8. Reevaluate strategy.

*The Informal Incremental Model.* Almost the opposite of the deliberate model, the *incremental school* treats strategy-making as evolving over time from innumerable decisions taken informally by organization members (Mintzberg, Ahlstrand, and Lampel, 2005; Bower and Gilbert, 2007; Pettigrew, 1985). Because these decisions are invariably political, the resulting alliances and compromises gradually give rise to a fragmented strategy. The incremental approach is highly involving and proceeds from the bottom up to create strategy. It reflects the following dynamics:

- Strategy evolves from inside the organization, not just from the market environment. Strategic decisions come from members within the firm in reacting to daily events.

- Strategy stems from values, traditions, and politics, not just from rational and formal analysis. Members are not always rational; they have vested interests and certain kinds of experience that bias their judgments in decision making.

- Strategy is a deeply ingrained pattern of behavior and cannot easily be turned off and on. It becomes embedded in the organization's practices and activities.

- Strategy emerges out of the cumulative effect of decisions and action taking. Each decision, when combined with other decisions, takes on a logical pattern of its own.

## Benefits and Costs

Each of these two approaches to involvement in strategy-making has pros and cons. The advantage of the deliberate model is its breadth in taking a comprehensive approach, ranging from markets to organization. Strategy comes from the plans made by experts, who presumably are in the best position to combine their experience and knowledge to take a broad look at the situation. The deliberate model takes a rational approach, unfolding in sequence where analysis precedes implementation, often calendar driven by considerations for the budget and capital expenditure cycle. A major weakness in the deliberate model is its formal sequence and rational structure, failing to take into account human behavior with its emotions, politics, and spontaneity affecting strategic decisions.

The strength of the incremental model is its descriptive realism rooted in the behavior and personalities of organization members whose self-interest and power positions affect strategic decisions. They also want to exercise their egos in finding ways to have their experience and knowledge respected and used. The weakness of the incremental model is its lack of comprehensiveness and rationality; it goes with the flow of emerging events and decisions without stopping to take a holistic and rational look at strategy. It can get lost in the trees and lose precious time.

Neither the deliberate nor the incremental approach is geared to cope with fast-moving events in today's world; each lacks urgency in practice. The deliberate model promotes long delays as consultants and planning staffs engage in lengthy data gathering and analytical studies, often overlooking the human factor. The political side of the incremental model can result in an endless series of compromises that obviate a coherent and holistic strategy.

## Guided Involvement as Synthesis

Guided involvement combines the two models, drawing on their advantages while correcting for their faults. It provides an organized context to deliberately address diverse and comprehensive content issues ranging from markets to organization. It also involves various individuals as they thoughtfully go about making decisions and ultimately reaching consensus. This kind of involvement serves to neutralize political behavior, overcoming resistance to build informed consensus and commitment throughout the organization. It also yields a type of strategy formation that, as Mintzberg and Waters (1985) put it, "walks on two feet, one deliberate, the other emergent" (p. 271).

Guided involvement includes providing the place and context within which members of a team can interact constructively. Jack Welch used guided involvement at GE when he engaged senior managers in strategic discussions at the firm's Crotonville training facility. Crotonville's classrooms provided a safe and sheltered context for Welch and about thirty to forty senior managers to openly discuss and debate strategic issues and make decisions about how to resolve them. This led to such programs as WorkOut and Six Sigma that involved the workforce in strategic change (Bartlett and Wozny, 2000).

As described in Appendix C, the Petrofuels Energy case contains an example of an organized retreat providing the context within which meaningful discussion and decision making can take place. (Actually, it is the only case we know of that tracks in detail the process of an off-site retreat describing how a top management team interacts during strategy-making.) Petrofuels established a deliberate context consisting of off-site retreats and facilitators to stimulate constructive discussion and the insight needed as top managers go about creating not only a strategy but an overall strategic system. This organized and guided process of rapidly reaching decisions that lead to an overall strategy is similar to what Malcolm Gladwell (2002) calls the *tipping point* in his book about "how little things can make a big difference." Microdecisions among managers in the retreat lead to macroresults in the form of a new strategic system and improved performance.

## Retreats as the Setting for *Dynamic Strategy-Making*

Off-site retreats help to accelerate guided involvement and real-time decision making. Issues can be quickly identified, content surfaced, and strategic decisions made with consensus.

Retreats help to frame a new direction and later to update it as events demand.

Some organizations try to hold strategy meetings at the office, but we find them to be nonproductive because of frequent interruption and a visible reminder of the status quo. Getting away helps to free up minds and allows people to reflect and discuss with greater objectivity. Many management groups hold retreats to discuss strategy, but these are usually dominated by the CEO and a few members, leading to serious dissatisfaction among other members. There are over fifteen books listed on Amazon about off-site retreats but none about conducting a strategy retreat, so the details of designing and leading a strategy retreat deserve close attention.

Many management groups try to make strategy on their own, without outside help, and they typically repeat past mistakes. This is where qualified consultants from outside or inside the firm can help to organize the agenda and facilitate discussions about strategy. Chapter Eight discusses this new kind of consulting role, the strategy facilitator, who organizes and enables constructive dialogue to take place rapidly among participants, leading to the creation of new strategic content and a strategic system.

## Logistics

It is essential that the CEO attend and participate. He or she must be included in preliminary planning for the retreat and should be listened to for suggestions. The CEO can be very helpful in making arrangements. First, there are the logistics and the schedule, and these can make a powerful difference in how well the sessions go:

- *Who should attend?* We prefer that no more than ten to fifteen people attend a strategy-making retreat, including all direct reports to the CEO, plus a few influential members from middle management, board, or staff.

- *Where should it be held?* A quiet but not too ostentatious site should be selected, preferably with lodging facilities. It should have a main meeting room as well as adjacent breakout rooms for subgroup meetings.

- *How long should it last?* Attempting to hold an off-site retreat for longer than three days is difficult because of pressing demands from the office. Also, minds start to wander at that point, and energy declines. Yet there is a minimum of one and one-half days, so there is at least one night to reflect and meet again the next morning.

- *How many retreats are necessary?* A final draft of the statement of strategic direction can be developed in two to three retreats separated by three or four weeks each, with everything completed within about six to ten weeks. It is a commitment of time away from work, and those participating should be ready to put in the effort. Not too much time should elapse between retreats, or momentum will suffer.

## The CEO's Role and Facilitator's Agenda

The facilitator briefs and consults with the CEO on how the retreat should be organized and agrees on the role the CEO should play at the retreat. The CEO may have strong ideas that need to be accepted or disabused. We suggest a limited role for the CEO, who should restrain his or her comments; talking too much may intimidate the group. However, there are crucial points where the CEO needs to intervene, especially when the group has trouble making a decision. This happened at the initial Petrofuels off-site retreat when the CEO, Wil Martin, intervened to correct the group's assumption that its only strategy was to generate cash to pay off interest on a huge debt accumulated by its parent headquarters. Martin interrupted the others, saying, "I feel that we can take control of our own destiny, no matter what the others say. Let's don't blame others for why we can't take control."

First, as facilitators, we explain the need to develop a strategic system and what that entails. As a result, the agenda is organized around the implementing format described in Chapter Six with its four essential elements that make up the statement of strategic direction: competitive logic, goals, organization, and action plan. The statement will contain managers' thoughts in writing about the four elements, beginning with the competitive logic. We make continuous use of subgroups with four to five people each to discuss each of the four elements. Small groups give more airtime and add perspective and help to validate conclusions when two groups agree.

The retreat should focus on strategic content, not on process like interpersonal feedback in team-building sessions. For us, a constructive process lies in how the quality of content is advanced by the agenda, leadership, and discussion. Lawler (2001) makes a similar argument. He advocates keeping the focus on business issues during high involvement:

> Basic to employee involvement in organizations is the shar-
> ing of information about business performance, plans, goals
> and strategies. Without business information, individuals cannot
> understand how the business is doing, nor can they make mean-
> ingful contributions to its success by participating in planning
> and setting direction [p. 29].

We believe that participants benefit by reading a few key articles on strategy-making prior to the first retreat, which gives them a conceptual context for addressing strategic content. Relevant readings might include Andrews's *Concept of Corporate Strategy* (1971), Porter's "What Is Strategy?" (1996), Hamel and Prahalad's "Strategic Intent" (1989), Eisenhardt and Sull's "Strategy as Simple Rules" (2008), and Beer and Eisenstat's "How to Have an Honest Conversation About Your Business Strategy" (2004).

## The First Retreat

Before the initial retreat, we ask participants to report their perceptions of strengths, weaknesses, opportunities, and threats as part of the traditional SWOT framework covered in Chapters Three and Five. This is typically done through personal interviews or e-mail, depending on time constraints. The well-known SWOT model provides a simple (but not overly simple) way for managers to express their opinions on the firm's current strategic situation. It is also good preparation for introduction of our 4D framework at the off-site retreat.

The CEO introduces the retreat and describes his or her role and that of the facilitators. The CEO needs to express his or her goal of producing a written, real-time strategic statement as a product of working together. The CEO should ask everyone to challenge their preconceptions and be willing to explore their opinions and suggestions openly.

As facilitators, we begin by describing the agenda; everyone is reminded that the schedule is flexible and open to change. Then we give our objectives: for them to create a written strategic statement composed of competitive logic, goals, organization, and action plan, which will result in a strategic system. Next, we present the SWOT findings to get the group immediately involved in discussion. We summarize the patterns appearing in the data and then ask how well our summary agrees with the group's impressions. This step usually results in a consensus that reduces disagreement later in the retreats. In addition, we briefly summarize what real-time strategy-making is all about, which updates their conceptual knowledge. This leads to the 4D model, which builds naturally off the SWOT findings and helps in preparing them to discuss competitive logic, the first essential element in the statement of strategic direction.

We describe the need to produce a written strategy statement organized around the four essential elements. We suggest that the statement should be worded as a set of specific guidelines, not a highly detailed planning document. Statements are typically formatted as bullet points on one to two pages. We then break the top team into subgroups and ask them to discuss and create the content of the competitive logic, which involves discovering a market opportunity that fits the firm's capabilities.

Here we find that the dialogue among members is likely more complex and uncertain than the discussion of the SWOT summary, but that is what we want. Finding the right fit between the organization and its environment is a creative act. Companies have many internal strengths and external opportunities to consider, not all of which will match up. For example, Petrofuels's leaders created their logic when they hit on the idea that customers might be willing to pay more for service and safety and that inefficient mom-and-pop competitors were unlikely to provide these features. The same kind of discovery process went on at the first retreat of the Near-Ritz hotel chain. Members concluded that they could build on the chain's strengths to grow throughout the southern United States and generate high profits by focusing on conferences and the business community. They rejected national or international expansion through acquisition because Near-Ritz lacked the know-how to pull that off successfully, even though it had the finances to make deals.

Initial ideas for a rough draft of the competitive logic are usually ready by the first evening, when a volunteer member can work on it and then read a draft for review the next morning. The team indicates areas of consensus and suggests any revisions. Once a draft of the logic has sufficient consensus, attention turns to goals that support the logic. On the last day in the last hour, the draft competitive logic and goals is read to the group for its final approval. Instructions are then given about how to secure feedback on the draft during the interim break. Top teams may be able to complete a draft of the entire strategy statement at the first retreat. In our experience, this is rare, and the remaining elements, organization and action plans, are typically addressed in the second retreat.

## Feedback After the First Retreat

Following the first off-site retreat, the draft of the competitive logic and goals is reviewed in subsequent interim meetings, led by senior executives from the first retreat, with middle managers and frontline employees for further discussion and feedback. These meetings start the involvement process by extending the strategy-making process out to the larger workforce, beginning with these four questions:

- Is the draft statement sufficiently realistic in its assumptions about the market?
- Do we have the capabilities to pull it off?
- Is it sufficiently inspirational, and will it win commitment?
- What suggestions would improve it?

In some cases, face-to-face feedback meetings may not be possible, and indirect methods for getting feedback will be necessary. Once, in a large professional association of eighteen thousand members, the draft statement was e-mailed to the leaders of its twenty-three divisions, who responded with comments, and the draft statement was greatly improved.

The reactions from these meetings are fed back to a designated member of the top team, who incorporates them into a redraft of the competitive logic and goals to be presented at the second off-site retreat. The period between the first and second off-site retreats gives senior managers time and feedback to reflect on their work and perform reality tests on the validity of assumptions in the statement.

## Second Retreat

The second off-site retreat is devoted to reviewing the feedback and finalizing the statement wording of competitive logic and the financial and rallying goals. If the intervening feedback and reflection time has led to significant doubts, it is probably best to start over. This rarely happens, however; small refinements are more the norm. The hope is that close to the final wording of the competitive logic and the goals can be completed by the end of the first day of the second retreat.

Then attention now turns to the other two remaining elements: organization and action plan. Without them, little will happen to turn the statement into reality. If the old organization remains intact, as some Petrofuels executives preferred, then employees are likely to behave in accordance with the old strategy. Without an action plan, implementation of the new strategy and strategic system will be haphazard and confusing.

We ask the subgroups to identify alternative organizational structures with pros and cons for each, including their preference for one, keeping in mind the need to ensure a close fit between the proposed structure and the competitive logic and goals. For example, Petrofuels's competitive logic required an emphasis on acquisitions, so during the organization discussion, the top team created a small acquisitions unit composed of a few skilled people. Politics is inherent in any organization discussion when the process of attaching names to boxes begins, so we recommend that the CEO, just as Wil Martin did at Petrofuels, take the recommended structure under advisement and then present a suggested organization, absent of names, to the team at the third off-site retreat.

Then the team identifies shared values that will guide employee behavior in a new strategic direction. These values should be in line with the tiebreakers in the competitive logic. Petrofuels's values included "unified teamwork, immediate service, and safety reputation," which later were translated into new behavior rules or social norms: "Don't be late on a delivery" and "Behave safety all the time." As for the people aspect of the organization, the top team identifies the required skills for new key jobs but avoids mentioning specific persons by name for political reasons, leaving those choices to the CEO and his or her team to meet privately after the final off-site retreat.

Just prior to the end of the second off-site retreat, the top team outlines an action plan for implementing the new strategy. At this time, only strategic initiatives are outlined; specific steps are postponed until the third off-site retreat. Initiatives appear rather logically after reflecting back on the first three elements. They are the answers to this question:

- What are the few priorities stemming from the competitive logic that will help us to move forward?

Adhering close to its competitive logic, Petrofuels created an initiative to market new tiebreakers of safety and service, so its action steps later became new trucks and training of the workforce. Again, team members are asked to review the most recent draft statement with their work teams before the third retreat. They are also asked to come to the retreat with specific steps to implement each initiative. Here are questions to ask:

- What resources are needed for what goals?
- Who will do what, when, and where?

## Third Retreat

At the third off-site retreat, final decisions on organization are made, steps under each initiative in the action plan are identified, and the final wording in the statement of strategic direction is approved. At Petrofuels's third retreat, the CEO presented a formal chart of a new organization structure to the group. Some members suggested minor changes, which Martin accepted. He then proposed an anonymous exercise that we've never seen before: he asked team members to write down on a piece of paper the job they wanted and, for each job, the person in the group they thought could best meet the requirements. Remarkably, after tabulation, there was exact agreement between the group and the job that each person wanted, except for Jack Davis, who wanted to hang on to his old operations job. Everyone thought

Jack would be good at leading the new marketing group. Rather than debate this problem in front of the group, Martin adjourned the meeting and went for a walk in the woods with Jack, asking him, "What will it take for you to accept the marketing job?" Jack replied that he wanted to recruit young graduates from his alma mater to work with him. Martin agreed. They came back to celebrate at dinner that evening.

The next morning, the Petrofuels team set specific steps for executing each initiative, a relatively easy task since many solutions had been suggested during the previous two retreats. Members had their own list of steps, and there was considerable overlap among them. The facilitators reminded them to make the actions consistent with what was required by the other three elements on the statement. At one point, there were too many initiatives, and members were asked to cut them back to something more realistic and manageable. The rest of the morning was devoted to agreeing on the final wording of the statement of strategic direction. This included adding in the initiatives and specific steps from the earlier discussion. After lunch, the agenda shifted to how to communicate the statement more widely to employees and involve them in moving ahead. We cautioned them against impersonal communications like e-mail, turning to more involving activities likely to evoke greater emotional commitment to the strategic direction, including celebrations, additional off-site retreats, and training sessions for the workforce.

## Follow-On Involvement

Guided involvement must continue after the last retreat, in a form suited to emerging events and the particular organization. For example, we helped Petrofuels create methods to keep the strategic changes moving ahead. A large celebration was held with a band, including a large banner with the rallying goal "Double in Five" on it. Each senior executive talked about what the new direction meant to him personally. A standing committee to oversee the change effort was created. It was composed of representatives from throughout the organization, reporting directly to the CEO every two weeks on progress. The CEO held frequent review meetings with his executive committee to assess if the strategic statement had taken hold and what else was needed to keep the momentum up.

Later, Wil Martin called for a fourth retreat of his executive team to address how to extend the change effort down to the lowest levels of the company. The facilitator moderated the meeting, although Martin and his team designed the agenda. During the meeting, the two remaining zone manager jobs in operations were eliminated and their job occupants transferred or retired. This removed one level from the field hierarchy, bringing CEO Martin closer to operations, which he wanted. Additional initiatives were launched, leading to several programs with different senior executives taking responsibility for each new program. For example, a training program was created for sales managers, and a sales incentive program was introduced. A new profit-sharing plan was also created for all employees. Finally, all store managers were invited to bring their best salesperson with them to a two-day conference in Denver, where Wil Martin discussed the company's strategic goals, followed by small group discussions and reports on how to implement the strategic statement in their daily behavior. Many good suggestions were received and accepted.

## Constructive and Productive Social Dialogue

From a process perspective, real-time strategy-making involves a good deal of sense making and social construction (Weick, 1995). Employees seek to arrive at sufficient consensus about the meaning of the company's strategic reality, resulting in agreement or disagreement about where the organization should be headed and how it will get there. This shared sense making occurs through *social dialogue* in which members intervene and interact to share their views about the organization and its environment, listen to each other, and reflect on the conclusions. Guided involvement facilitates positive and productive social dialogue among team members. It promotes open sharing of views, active listening to members' opinions, and joint reflection on what has been said and discussed. Guided involvement organizes members' discussions based on 4D analysis and focuses them on the four essential elements of the statement of strategic direction. It helps participants interact and reflect rapidly. Nothing constructive will happen without productive social dialogue, which reveals where everyone stands and what content they want for a future strategic system.

## Intellectual and Emotional Aspects

Social dialogue has intellectual and emotional sides. Ideas and emotions serve to engage and stimulate others—or they can result in conflicts that stop the dialogue. Because emotions like fear, anger, relief, enthusiasm, and other emotions can make or break strategy-making, guided involvement promotes skillful listening and respect for others' ideas. It helps participants feel secure enough to speak up and engage each other with their opinions; it may even help them have a "good fight" (Eisenhardt, Kahwajy, and Bourgeois, 1997). Members can disagree openly as long as they respect each other in doing so.

Guided involvement begins by using the 4D framework and four key elements to break participants out of habitual ways of thinking, resulting in fresh insights and feelings. The presence of a skillful CEO and consultant facilitator is invaluable for keeping social dialogue on a constructive course. The consultant is more on the deliberate side, providing structure and a topical focus to move the discussion forward, while the CEO is more on the emergent side, with interventions to enhance progress. Most of the following examples involve interventions and interactions by CEO Wil Martin as he tries to guide his group through the strategy making.

## Examples of Productive Dialogue

Following are some concrete examples of productive social dialogue involving Petrofuels's CEO, top team, and workforce. All of them contain both cognition and emotion as the strategy and the strategic system is advanced to fruition.

**The CEO reflects on the budget meetings before the strategy process begins.**

> It was an excellent forum that enabled me to ask questions, and that's why I enjoyed it. Very quickly, I learned a lot about the company. We came up with a laundry list of key issues, and airing them was a major improvement even though we couldn't solve all of them. What came out of all this was a commitment to achieve our profit goal for the year—and to hell with whether it was the right level; we would still try to achieve it.

These meetings helped Martin learn more about the company and build a relationship with his top team. Note that he asks questions and encourages input, which makes his team feel valued. He is relaxed about solving problems, and this attitude carries over to the team. He leads them to a point where the team members emotionally commit to achieve a short-term budget goal. They end up exceeding the goal, and this accomplishment solidifies Martin in their eyes as a leader who can now ask them to engage in a strategy process, something they had not done before.

**The CEO intervenes to move events forward after the SWOT analysis at the first retreat.**

CEO Martin: Why do you guys see so many threats and so few opportunities?

March (vice president of transportation): Because the market for petrofuel is so mature and customers for petrofuel are limited.

Cook (vice president of supply): Besides, even if we could sell more petrofuel, we don't have enough money for investments because all our cash goes to Global Services to pay off interest on its large debt.

CEO Martin: I feel that we can take control of our own destiny, no matter what others say. Let's don't blame others for why we can't take control. I have no hidden agenda for what we might discover.

Here we see Martin exercising his leadership and intervention skills. He reassures the group that he has no hidden agenda, so they are free to think of strategic alternatives and ways of getting there. He directs the group to look to the future, stop feeling constrained by limits around them, and assume responsibility in taking control of their own destiny.

**The management team makes a breakthrough insight later in the first retreat.**

At the end of the second day, each subgroup presented surprisingly similar words for their competitive logic and goals. They seemed to agree that Petrofuels should, as they said, "concentrate exclusively on the petrofuel industry," "become more marketing oriented," "make acquisitions," and "set high financial goals." The subgroup discussions had determined that Petrofuels, despite being in a mature industry, could still "clean up," as one member put it, because its major competitors were "badly managed" and there were many small "mom-and-pop operations that might sell out."

The remaining discussion centered on how high their financial goals should be; the central concern was how Petrofuels could still generate cash for Global Services while also making investments in acquisitions and additional marketing programs. A way out of this dilemma was found when one member proposed selling off nonpetrofuel assets, closing down low-profit Petrofuels outlets, and cutting operating costs. When another member suggested that the company should try to "double profits in five years," Wil Martin said, "I could get very excited by that goal, and I know I can sell it to Global Services."

The off-site retreat ended on Sunday with Wil Martin complimenting the group and leading them in a discussion about follow-up steps. It was agreed that each person should meet in pairs with middle managers, get feedback, and then draft a separate strategy statement to be given to another member, Bill Hope, for final drafting of a single statement. Martin asked that the final draft be "subjected to some hard market and financial analysis." Martin then announced that the group should meet again in three weeks for a second off-site retreat to "ratify a new strategy statement and resume the discussion on organization structure." These interactions show how discussions in two subgroups came up with the same strategy of staying focused on petrofuels while proposing additional actions to strengthen their market position. The CEO encouraged them and gave instructions for how to move forward.

**The CEO comments to the consultant before the third retreat.**

> We need to move these meetings off the discussion level and into action. I'm ready to move, and the group seems ready too. They seem to be waiting for me to make a decision, so I will do it. All our financial and marketing checks on the strategy statement make sense, and the middle managers like it. They say it isn't us now, so the question centers on implementation—especially organization structure and who fills what jobs.

Martin decided to invite only the four senior vice presidents of the major functions to the off-site retreat because "these guys are more crucial to making this happen, and I have to focus on their anxieties."

**The CEO speaks to senior vice presidents about positions in the new organization at the third retreat.**

When Wil Martin had finished his presentation on organization structure to the four senior vice presidents, he invited them to "criticize my proposal for how well it implements our new strategy.... Feel free to shoot holes in it." After agreeing on a new structure with the senior vice presidents moving to new positions, Martin said: "I'm ready to go with all of you in new positions, so let's toast our goal of doubling over the next five years and all of us having a lot of fun doing it."

In this example, Wil Martin is orchestrating his top team to focus on action taking and puts his stamp on the strategy statement. He also realizes the group cannot make a decision on organization because of members' vested interests, so he decides to propose a new organization structure. He reduces the size of the group to his four senior vice president operating heads to avoid political difficulties and continues with his openness by inviting criticism of his proposal. He finishes the discussion with positive comments about moving forward.

**The workforce reactions to their managers' new leadership are positive.**
Two long-tenured employees had this to say about their new bosses:

> Before Wil Martin, the guys at the head office rarely ever visited my workplace, and then it was to find something wrong. Now I feel like they are actually trying to help me. My sales have gone up a lot, and my paycheck is a lot fatter too.

> I was just about ready to leave when the lights came on. I got a new boss who finally listened to me. He was giving me a lot more work than I had before.

These reactions show the constructive side of social dialogue —how new openness and team action at the top are being modeled by lower-level managers. Martin set the tone, and his managers emulated him. The strategic effort at Petrofuels was broadening out to affect the behavior and attitudes of the entire workforce.

## Some Cautions Regarding Involvement and Constructive Dialogue

Even when real-time demands are pressing on the organization, the purpose of guided involvement is to promote thoughtful and deliberate discussion, not to rush everyone to conclusion or force decisions without signs of consensus. And surprises can happen during open discussion; people will come up with new ideas that threaten the status quo, provoking resistance from some. This occurred in the Petrofuels case when executive Jack Davis resisted taking on the marketing job. Some members of the team became angry with him, but with active and skillful intervention, the CEO won Jack over. In the end, leadership quality makes a difference in real-time strategy-making, the subject of the next chapter as we focus on capable strategic leaders and the change process.

# 8

# LEADING, CHANGING, AND FOLLOWING-UP IN REAL TIME

As the previous chapter shows, skillful strategic leadership is crucial to implementing *dynamic strategy-making*. It provides the direction, motivation, and reinforcement for assessing the organization and implementing and revising a new strategy. Indeed, the strategic system will not get off the ground without effective strategic leadership throughout the organization, from top leaders to frontline managers. They must all behave like strategic leaders, providing a role model for the behavior that is expected, along with training and developing others, providing feedback on progress, and suggesting improvements.

*Dynamic strategy-making* means continuous change. All new strategies involve changes in how members think and behave at work, which can be resisted or turned into positive momentum. Strategic leaders must remain vigilant and proactive, looking for what needs to be done to ease the path forward, being alert to overcome blockages that can delay or even undo a real-time strategy. It also requires continuous adjustments in strategic content based on feedback from employees. When initiatives and goals are accomplished, new ones must be added to the strategic statement and implemented throughout the organization.

In the following section, we describe the capabilities contributing to effective strategic leadership, particularly at the senior level, where strategy-making starts. We then turn to the special role of the CEO or other senior leader who is ultimately responsible for ensuring that the strategic system is designed, launched, and continually revitalized in a process of strategic change. Finally, we describe the functions of strategic leadership that need to occur with other managers throughout the organization.

# I. LEADING
## Strategic Leader Capabilities

Often there is a large gap between strategic intentions and the leadership capability to make them happen (Hsieh and Yik, 2005): "The best planned strategy is no more than wishful thinking if it can't be translated from concept to reality—why do so many companies discover their leadership shortfall only when executing their strategies?" (p. 69).

As mentioned in prior chapters, responsibility for creating a dynamic strategic system falls on the senior leadership team. Research (Greiner and Bhambri, 1989) suggests that much hinges on two characteristics of senior leaders who lead the change:

- Leaders' *cognitive ability* to think about strategic content in comprehensive ways, ranging from analysis of markets to the organization. If their mind-sets are narrow, leaders are likely to run into trouble; myopic thinkers tend to overlook key factors bearing on what leads to strategic success.
- Leaders' *behavioral style*, which should be more collaborative rather than unilateral. A collaborative style is more likely to elicit solid input about, acceptance of, and commitment to the strategic system from others in the organization.

These two factors contribute in their mix to two very different types of leaders: the *pragmatist*, who tends to think about strategy rather narrowly and acts unilaterally, as contrasted with the *visionary*, who conceives strategy broadly and leads collaboratively. Each style has advantages and drawbacks, and leaders must combine them in order to move strategy forward.

## Pragmatists

Most people are rewarded and move up in their early careers because of what they do pragmatically in solving daily problems and improving performance. So when most become senior managers, they tend to think about strategy in a narrow, today-oriented mode, looking for issues to be solved immediately. They often favor formal methods looking for data to back up their conclusions. Sometimes they engage in firefighting to solve a strategic issue, hoping it will go away with short-term solutions. Pragmatic leaders tend to:

- Solve daily problems and make decisions
- Meet formally with immediate subordinates
- Act rational and cool
- Focus on weaknesses
- Talk about current issues
- Follow up on decisions

As a result, they are often good implementers but can get lost among the trees of the broader forest. However, the today mode in thinking and behavior is an advantage in real-time strategy-making.

## Visionaries

These leaders are good at thinking about and advocating a vision and future for the organization. They get out of their offices and talk a lot with employees about the strengths and values of the firm. Visionary leaders tend to:

- Advocate values, goals, vision, and direction
- Make contact with employees at all levels
- Act warm, expressive, and supportive
- Pay attention to strengths of the business
- Talk about future goals

Their weakness lies in not recognizing immediate problems and not being able to step back from their long-term vision to focus on the practical details of formulating strategic content involving markets, competitors, and products, as well as the often difficult process of implementation. Their broader viewpoint is an advantage when it comes to strategic content.

## Effective Strategic Leadership

From our experience, capable strategic leaders combine pragmatist and visionary qualities in their thinking and behavior. Their visionary side enables them to think comprehensively about a desirable future in clear, positive terms that motivate others to go where they haven't been before. It helps them to be highly visible in extolling the new strategic direction and behaving accordingly. Senior leaders must also display pragmatic qualities, however. At times they need to be standing solidly on both feet, attending to the details of forming and implementing the content of a strategy, while holding others accountable for achieving results on time. "Walking the talk" is essential to gain credibility for the new strategy in the organization and to not appear hypocritical.

Wil Martin showed pragmatism at Petrofuels Energy during his first six months on the job when he addressed pressing budgetary problems. And when executives exceeded budget goals, Martin also acted as a visionary, giving gold clocks as a symbol of what could be accomplished by the team in a short time frame. Similarly, Jack Welch was a visionary by being out-front with employees in talking up the strengths of various GE divisions and also acted as the pragmatist when he initiated the WorkOut and Six Sigma programs (Bower and Dial, 1994; Bartlett and Wozny, 2000).

Of course, not everyone in top management has these capabilities or can easily acquire them. And it is very difficult to transform a dedicated "bluebird" (a visionary) into a "woodpecker" (pragmatist), or vice versa. But if the composition of top teams includes a good mixture of both approaches, members can combine their different styles to achieve a positive overall effect. They can perform complementary roles, some leading the more visionary activities and others leading more on implementation. A capable CEO or consultant can also mentor one-sided leaders on how to express more of the qualities they may not have and tend to ignore.

## CEO Turnover

New CEOs no longer enjoy the traditional honeymoon year in which to study the organization and get acquainted before being judged on results. CEO succession can be crucial, especially in firms requiring strategic change, when a top leader must be found with both visionary and pragmatic skills. Regrettably, often little attention is paid by those selecting a new CEO, with the appointment going almost routinely and ritually to the next in line. A recent survey (Bower, 2007) shows that 85 percent of CEO replacements come from within the organization, and over 50 percent are next in line, with all of them serving more than ten years within the firm. These "new" internal CEOs have long been conditioned by the past strategy and likely will not rock the boat. Before Jack Welch became CEO at GE, he was a dark horse, not next in line, and was selected after interviews by the board, which considered several candidates. He was what Bower (2007) calls an "inside outsider." Lou Gerstner came to IBM from the outside to transform it from hardware to services; outsiders are known for making more changes than insiders, though most stumble because of not knowing and winning support in the organization, as happened to Jack Anderson at Coast Yellow Pages.

Unfortunately, in addition to being hard to find, new CEOs are hard to keep. CEO turnover is more frequent than in the past; almost two-thirds of the world's companies have changed CEOs at least once in the past five years. According to Denis St.-Amour, president of the human resource consulting firm DBM's Center for Executive Options in New York, executives are typically "gone in three years—not necessarily because they're not doing the right thing, but because they're not doing it fast enough." In other words, CEOs may have trouble keeping pace with strategy-making in a 24/7 world. This is in contrast to CEO Wil Martin at Petrofuels, who as a new CEO didn't stop to go out to visit the field and begin a year of study; instead, he began immediate meetings with his team and succeeded in getting them to make up a budget shortfall, an accomplishment that gave him sufficient credibility to launch a strategic change process.

## II. CHANGING
### The CEO's Role in Strategic Change

CEOs must be out front in creating, executing, and revising strategic content. They must "behave the strategy" and hold others accountable for doing so. Some organizations appoint a chief strategy officer (CSO) to take over for the CEO and perform these roles (Breene, Nunes, and Hill, 2007). We strongly believe that the CEO *is* the CSO and that the CEO role in strategy-making cannot be outsourced or delegated. To delegate strategy-making sends the wrong signal to organization members; it confuses them about who is in charge of the firm's strategy and raises serious questions about how committed the CEO is to the strategy. The role of CSO can't be outsourced beyond the CEO (Montgomery, 2008).

Any new strategy requires strategic change. In fast-paced environments, CEOs must frequently create and implement new strategies or at least make constant changes to them. This requires special attention to the leadership roles needed to move the organization through different stages or phases of strategic change. It also demands skillful attention to the power and politics that invariably arise when change occurs. *Dynamic strategy-making* is consistent with these stages and speeds them up.

A great deal has been written about strategic change, mainly from effort to break "brain maps" that cause people to hold on to the status quo (Black and Gregersen, 2002), or new methods on how to move ahead with major change (Kotter and Cohen, 2002). Although this information is useful for managing change, it provides little guidance to top leaders about what roles they need to play at different times in the change process.

## The Phases for Achieving Strategic Change

We have developed a dynamic model that identifies six sequential phases generally needed to achieve strategic change. These phases overlap with each other in practice; they are described next, along with the specific roles CEOs need to play at each stage to move the organization forward. The first two phases deal with supporting conditions needed to initiate strategic change, and the remaining four are concerned with designing and leading the change process. CEOs need to address these phases, tailor them to their situation, and perform the requisite roles to lead change successfully:

1. *Design the entry context: The CEO as negotiator of a mandate for a new strategy.* CEOs must gain approval and support to move ahead from key stakeholders, such as the board of directors, union officials, or significant customers. Unfortunately some CEOs never get this support, and strategic change never takes off, as Jack Anderson discovered at Coast Yellow Pages. At Petrofuels, CEO Wil Martin sought approval from the chairman of Global Services for his efforts to change strategy and received it.

2. *Achieve early positive impact: The CEO as results-oriented manager.* This phase, particularly important for new CEOs, helps them build credibility in the organization through demonstrating that they can obtain performance results. It gives them needed influence to launch strategic change, especially when members have concerns about setting

out on a highly uncertain adventure. CEO Wil Martin gained credibility at Petrofuels by making and exceeding the budget goals during his first three months on the job. This accomplishment added credibility in the eyes of his subordinates and allowed him to initiate the strategy process.

3. *Create competitive logic: The CEO as visionary.* This phase creates the strategic content related to the firm's market position and business model. CEOs need to create an open dialogue where other senior leaders share their own visions, and perhaps synthesize a competitive logic not previously considered. Petrofuels began this step in the first workshop, where a new competitive logic was based on outcompeting small and inefficient mom-and-pop firms by adding features of service and safety in return for charging a slightly higher price.

4. *Fit people with positions: The CEO as political orchestrator.* In many cases, a new strategic direction will require reassigning or hiring personnel to fill new jobs. CEOs must be sensitive to the political ramifications of moving people around in the organization and take appropriate steps to deal with these. Petrofuels's management restructured the organization with new acquisitions and marketing groups, all staff functions under one person. It reduced twenty-four area managers to fourteen. In the end, thirty-nine managers changed jobs. Not everyone was happy with these changes, and CEO Wil Martin had to persuade some to accept them, as he did with Jack Davis by taking a walk in the woods.

5. *Mobilize energy: The CEO as communicator of commitment.* This step involves getting lower levels of management on board with the new strategic content. Generally various forums need to be held to openly discuss the new strategic direction to determine if managers think it is realistic

and can get excited about implementing it. Feedback may point out a need to modify the statement of strategic direction. Wil Martin held a series of meetings. Once the team had prepared the strategic statement, he arranged for a celebration and launch of the new strategic system, with the rallying goal "Double in Five."

6. *Alter workforce skills and behavior: The CEO as architect of empowerment.* This phase is critical to getting the broader workforce on board and behaving in accordance with the new strategy. It may require considerable communication and training to ensure that members of the workforce understand the strategic content and gain the skills and expertise to enact it behaviorally. They also need to be given sufficient information and autonomy to respond rapidly to emergent events. At Petrofuels, truck drivers went through extensive retraining on providing service to customers, wearing new uniforms, driving their newly painted trucks, and how to deliver on time. Profit sharing was extended to the workforce as a reward for performance.

It is important to note that these phases may not apply when organizations are headed rapidly downhill and may need serious restructuring, cost cutting, and replacing personnel. Such drastic efforts will stabilize the firm, however. Once the organization is on solid footing, CEOs need to start the phases of strategic change that will get it growing again. The turnaround problems of downward spiraling organizations are legend in the literature (Amburgey, Kelly, and Barnett, 1993). Most do not survive despite herculean resuscitation efforts.

## Breaking the Hold of Politics

CEOs must be skillful at using power and politics in creating a united and committed team behind the strategy. For example, the

CEO of Petrofuels invited only the four senior vice presidents to the final retreat so as to reduce the size to avoid political resistance from some of the staff he wanted to work under one senior vice president so that he could spend more time on operations. He let each know ahead of time what he was going to do and listened to their comments about the change.

Power and politics often carry a negative image in the popular management press. Yet their use is not inherently negative, especially if applied constructively to make real-time strategy happen (Pfeffer, 1992). Any change in strategy can easily threaten the existing power structure, resulting in resistance from some members who favor the status quo and engage in endless debates that delay and may even water down the full impact of a new strategy (Hickson and others, 1986). And there are senior executives who do not respect their CEO and covertly undermine his or her authority.

Unfortunately, there are plenty of CEOs with insufficient power and credibility to deal with political dynamics. Gamma Bank is a prime example of this; there, as we noted in Chapter Two (and as Appendix B describes further), two peers were competing for the chairman's job, but the chairman believed in survival of the fittest and was reluctant to intervene.

Figure 8.1 depicts four political behaviors that arise from CEO and manager interaction in top management teams engaged in strategy-making (Greiner and Schein, 1989). To deal effectively with political behavior, CEOs need to move their team rapidly toward *active consensus*. This requires CEOs to assert influence in getting team members to willingly join with them in creating a new strategy. According to consultant-professor David Nadler, CEO of Delta Consulting, who has worked with over fifty CEOs in strategic change: "The CEO should make it transparently clear to his team members when he wants decisions reached by consensus and when he wants to make them alone. This way, everyone knows where they stand, the CEO included. The CEO will also benefit by putting himself in the position of team builder."

## Figure 8.1 Strategy and Political Behavior in Top Management Teams

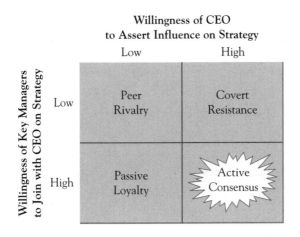

It is very hard to do real-time strategy-making when there is peer rivalry (as at Gamma Bank), passive loyalty, or covert resistance in the team (as at Coast Yellow Pages). Peer rivalry is common in new management teams when cohesion is likely to be low and members' egos drive interaction. Here, CEOs need to assert their influence to build the team and focus it on substantive strategy issues. They also need to assert influence when there is passive loyalty, which can lead to considerable delay and frustration as members wait loyally for the CEO to act. This often happens in entrepreneurial companies when the CEO has hired most of the top managers who are either family members or outsiders loyal and grateful for their careers.

*Covert resistance*, difficult to detect, can subtly sabotage the strategy-making process, as it did at Coast Yellow Pages with the cooked figures to back the Rescope case. CEOs need to fight the natural tendency to overestimate their influence with members; they need to actively listen and skillfully probe team members about their willingness to engage in strategy-making. When Wil Martin arrived at Petrofuels, it was likely in a state of covert resistance to the previous CEO. It took Martin three months to gain sufficient credibility and power from achieving short-term goals before he was able to begin the strategy process and move toward active consensus.

In addition to applying their own political skills, CEOs can draw on special processes and consulting expertise to move the top team toward active consensus. In Chapter Seven, we developed the guided involvement process for off-site retreats to help teams surface strategic issues, openly discuss them, and create consensus about strategic content. We also discovered a new type of consultant, the *strategy facilitator*, who is geared to helping top teams create and execute real-time strategy (described in Chapter Nine). Strategy facilitators organize and guide teams while focusing on the substance of strategic content and not letting negative emotions distort the discussion and possibly doom progress.

Differences among managers over strategic content are a normal part of strategy-making, but they are likely amenable to resolution after thoughtful discussion and new facts are exposed. We saw this happen when Wil Martin proposed that his team entertain the possibility of a new strategy for Petrofuels, but members of his management team disagreed because they viewed their jobs only as generating cash to their parent company. Then, after further debate and discussion, they discovered a way forward while generating even more cash from greatly increased profits.

## III. FOLLOWING-UP
### Extending Strategic Leadership

Strategy-making needs to extend downward and outward to all levels of management and the workforce. It won't become a real-time strategic system unless the workforce is highly involved. Everyone needs to understand and commit to the new strategic direction. Strategy will remain an empty abstraction unless employees are involved in translating strategic content into their

telling the middle to get the bottom involved. This guarantees that nothing positive will happen.

Once empowered, the workforce, including managers and frontline employees, may not know what to do with their new responsibilities. They will require a lot of training and reeducation; after all, strategic change requires behavior change. Managers must learn how to delegate and workers how to provide direct and honest feedback. Besides training, the workforce must be supported by having the right information at the right time to mount rapid, effective responses. They must train members how to make good decisions and reward them for their achievements.

The top leaders at Petrofuels pursued many ways to involve and empower the workforce. They began with a reality check to review a draft statement of strategic direction with groups of middle managers and later incorporated several more steps, such as establishing a strategy review committee composed of representative levels and leading an off-site retreat with frontline employees.

## Redesigning Systems

Several formal systems need to be changed and redesigned to reinforce the new strategy in the behavior of all employees. The reward systems should be changed to promote strategic behavior. Rewards aren't just money; they can also be symbolic, as when Wil Martin at Petrofuels awarded his top team with gold clocks for accomplishing the budget. He also arranged for them to receive added bonuses from the chairman of Global Systems, and a new profit-sharing system was established for first-level employees.

The information systems need to measure strategic progress toward financial and rallying goals set in the strategy statement. Data that measure progress on initiatives need to be collected and distributed (Kaplan and Norton, 2008). Information must be in real time too. At Near-Ritz, CEO Alice Smith asked the information technology group to report room revenues each day for each hotel by 5:00 P.M. The group made the system work—a symbolic act that sent a message to the organization that increased marketing effort on a daily basis was important if each hotel was to reach its financial goal of 30 percent net operating profit within two years.

The talent system needs to identify and develop leaders and employees who model the values and expectations set by the strategic system. Training in the new strategy and the behaviors needed to enact it is essential.

## Communicating Constantly

Consistent with seeking employee input, strategic leaders need to communicate constantly to keep the workforce informed about how strategy-making is progressing. Quick and reliable information can help to squelch rumors, which abound in strategic change. It can inspire and motivate employees by providing them with data they need to engage meaningfully in the process.

Communication can take many forms, from informal meetings with work teams to town hall gatherings with larger groups. Whatever the form, communication of the strategy should be worded, according to Heath and Heath (2007), as a "sticky idea": "Employees need to understand what your organization stands for, where it's headed, and what will make it successful. In other words they need to be able to 'talk strategy.' And if they can talk strategy back to you, you'll benefit from insights that otherwise be untapped and invisible" (p. 253).

The management at Petrofuels accomplished this by holding a memorable celebration to announce key elements and excerpts from its statement of strategic direction. It included banners with "Double in Five" on it, and a band. Wil Martin and all his senior executives spoke to the workforce about their commitment to the company's goals and future direction.

CEOs must be able to articulate the strategy in clear, understandable terms that inspire their employees. In the Near-Ritz hotel chain, the workforce was energized by hearing the CEO personally talk about the meaning and implications of the new strategy at several regional meetings. Attendees from different levels in each hotel met in small groups to identify gaps between what the statement said and actual practice, and they proposed solutions to close the gap. The CEO's talk was recorded on videotape so it could be shown and discussed in every hotel in the chain.

Feedback must also be institutionalized through adding formal arrangements to promote and reinforce follow-up. As we have indicated, a strategy review group can be appointed with rotating members who are representative of different levels in the organization. This group should meet monthly, followed by a subsequent meeting with the CEO to report their conclusions. The CEO should set aside time in meetings with the executive team to remind them of the strategy and how their decisions must remain consistent with the direction of the strategic system.

## Revising Constantly

*Dynamic strategy-making* is not a one-time event with a predictable yearly review. It is a way of life—an ongoing process that constantly revises strategic content to keep pace with the changing environment. Strategic leaders must design and direct this feedback adjustment process, which needs to take place throughout the organization. They need to constantly monitor how well the strategy is being executed and how well it continues to fit the competitive environment. One way to accomplish this is through a group of rotating members who report to the CEO to meet and assess data coming from an information system that measures progress from implementing initiatives and accomplishing goals.

Leaders need to be able to use this information to change the content of the strategic system. In essence, they need to create an effective organizational learning process in which members learn how to enact and revise the strategy by trying to execute it, learning from the results, making necessary revisions, and so on indefinitely. Over time, members improve their learning capability to change and improve the organization. In fast-paced environments, this can be a key source of competitive advantage. At Petrofuels, Wil Martin held a monthly meeting with a permanent standing strategy review committee composed of members from several levels of the organization. The committee constantly reviewed and adjusted strategic content as the circumstances demanded and as goals and initiatives were accomplished.

## From Executives to Consultants

As we have seen in this chapter, strategic leadership is an everyday event and encompasses more than solving problems as they arise. The strategic statement should be used consistently to guide the management team in daily behavior and decisions.

Often when it comes to developing a new strategy, CEOs turn to consultants for additional expertise. In Chapter Nine, we look at different approaches to strategy consulting, including a new kind of consultant, the strategy facilitator, who is especially useful when helping to install a real-time strategic system that becomes a permanent system for continuous revision in its content. Unlike many other consultants, strategy facilitators leave behind the learning and skills so the client won't need future consulting help on strategy.

# 9

## FACILITATING REAL-TIME STRATEGY

### A New Role for Consultants

Senior executives are not accustomed to making strategy every day. Indeed, they spend less time on strategy than other activities: surveys show an average of 10 to 15 percent of senior management's annual workload is on strategy. Unfortunately, many CEOs and organizations, not yet recognizing the demands of a 24/7 world, still adhere to traditional status quo planning practices without seeking outside help. They repeat past mistakes by continuing to use conventional and bureaucratic planning approaches, such as once-a-year calendar-driven plans linked to budgets and capital expenditures.

These mistakes often happen because senior executives are unable to break away from ritualistic practices. For example, several Petrofuels Energy managers didn't see much promise in working on strategy when their product was mature and all they had to do was generate cash for the parent to pay off interest on the debt. Fortunately, the new CEO, with the help of a facilitator, encouraged further discussion where they began to see the "old" business in a new light.

For leaders who dare let go of the past and hope to keep up with a 24/7 world, five options are available. The easiest four have the least potential: (1) pursue pseudo strategy-making on an ad hoc issue basis, (2) perform surgery by hiring a new CEO as savior, (3) add a CSO (chief strategy officer) to their corporate staff, or (4) engage a conventional strategy consulting firm for an expert study and advice.

None of these alternatives stands much of a chance of success for making a real-time adjustment. Pseudo strategy-making is superficial and temporary. Many new CEOs end up in failure, as happened at Coast Yellow Pages where a new CEO didn't survive to see his long-term vision realized. Internal CSOs, being senior and usually hired from a conventional consulting firm, run the risk of not knowing much about *dynamic strategy-making*. Conventional consulting firms are likely to conduct lengthy studies, taking all the expertise when they leave, causing the client no option but to summon the consultants again in the future.

The fifth and best alternative, we think, for adapting to a fast-paced world is what we call *strategy facilitation*. It is a new type of consulting that has emerged to help management teams do real-time strategy-making. It employs a very different approach from conventional consulting. As we have shown, it isn't vision setting or a mission defining exercise. It uses high-involvement methods to develop and inform strategic content decisions and thereby create a real-time strategic system. Strategy facilitation is now being offered by larger firms like Delta Consulting and is often practiced by small boutique firms and independent consultants.

CEOs and organizations are not aware about how to do *dynamic strategy-making*. Only by building this capability into the firm will their efforts at strategy-making keep up with the rest of the world. They will need help initially in setting up a strategic system, and then they can continuously use guided involvement to revise, add, and remove strategic content. With practice, they will learn how to maintain and sustain an effective and living strategic system that permeates the organization.

This is our goal in working with clients—and hopefully to work ourselves out of a job. We provide strategy facilitation to help clients learn how to do *dynamic strategy-making*. And they learn by doing it. We provide useful frameworks and a format for writing down and setting strategic direction while using guided involvement. These methods help clients create a lasting strategic system, and in the process they learn independently how to do real-time strategy-making themselves in the future.

In this chapter, we define and describe strategy facilitation and go on to contrast it with other types of strategy consulting. We conclude with advice to clients who must select facilitators from all the look-alike consultants coming before them and go on to manage them effectively. Clients need to become wiser as they go about searching for and interviewing strategy consultants. And more consultants need to build strategy facilitation into their skill set.

## Other Types of Consulting

Other approaches to strategy consulting are very different from strategy facilitation. They fall into two long-standing and contrasting types. *Conventional strategy consulting* is practiced mostly by established and traditional consulting firms that do large-scale strategy projects involving intensive data-gathering studies and detailed recommendations. *Organization development (OD)/human resource (HR) consulting* is performed by big consulting firms or small consulting boutiques. OD/HR consulting can use strategy retreats to set a vision for the future direction of their organizations. These two approaches have different conceptions of strategy and different approaches to intervention.

### Conventional Strategy Consulting

A variety of firms specializing in this approach pursue a range of issues. Many take a market-focused view toward strategy formulation based on analytical studies with field data, ending with formal recommendations. Other consulting firms take an internal look at leadership and the organization to examine how the organization formulates strategy and goes about executing it. The consulting divisions of accounting and computer firms with small strategy formulation groups are mainly tactical, emphasizing the use of information systems and technology to solve such issues as outsourcing, value chain analysis, operations improvement, internal systems design, and Web development.

All these consulting firms have several commonalities in their scale of operations. The large ones seek out large global clients that can be served worldwide on the same project by consultants from their internationally located offices. They have expensive payrolls and overheads, leading to high total fees for projects that stretch over several months and run into multimillions of dollars. Typically these firms earn their revenues through billing for time spent on big projects, so the incentive is to chalk up lots of study or implementing time in return for added revenue. Sometimes the rate is adjusted for perceived value to the client. In addition, there are small consulting firms, staffed mainly by alumni from the larger firms, that are less expensive, emphasizing personal service to local clients.

Conventional strategy consulting firms typically supplement their extensive data-gathering using their own in-house analytical models. They examine the structure of markets and the economics of competition, believing that statistical facts and data modeling will enlighten strategy formulation and persuade the client (Stern and Deimler, 2006). Other firms look inside organizations at strategy execution, assessing how the firm is organized and led, the efficiency of the information and production systems, and the compensation of executives (Rasiel and Friga, 2002).

Conventional strategy consulting often fails to respond to clients' real-time needs. Data-gathering takes too long, and the reports are either written or formal slide shows, treating managers as a passive audience. Their methods do not actively involve executives from the outset; instead, manager participation is limited to being selectively interviewed as a small sample, receiving interim feedback presentations, and attending final meetings at which they hear recommendations—just as the consultants behaved at Gamma Bank. Study content is controlled by the consultants, causing their findings, conclusions, and reports to be of their own making. The biggest downside is that the client doesn't learn the skills and knowledge of how to do more effective strategy-making—other than to call in the consultants again, and by the time they complete their study, the opportunities are long gone.

The above approach is illustrated by wording on the Web site of a leading strategy consulting firm headquartered in Europe. It single-handedly does the analysis, finds opportunities, and offers solutions—despite advocating close teamwork:

> Our task is to find solutions and uncover opportunities that will deliver winning competitive positions and superior returns. Every strategic challenge is special; each response is unique. We research, analyze and implement with pace and creativity. We approach problems from all angles in order to provide our clients with the answers they need. We believe in teamwork, working closely with our clients at every stage to deliver outstanding results.

Recently, many conventional firms have shifted focus away from strategy formulation to emphasize strategy tactics. They address such issues as merger search and integration, succession planning, outsourcing, information system design, value-chain analysis, market research, compensation, and product design and innovation. For these projects, consultants send a team to the client to apply their valuable technical expertise, like the design and implementation of a new information system. They usually accept the client's overall strategy as given by addressing how to implement strategic initiatives more efficiently. One leading firm describes several such tactical projects on its Web site as representative of its "strategy practice": "Our consultants reviewed the client's existing distribution capabilities, marketing efforts and competitive position. They found that while marketing managers closely monitored the needs of customers, the needs of the sales channel were less well understood."

To be sure, conventional strategy studies, such as the above example, can be helpful as informational input to a real-time strategy-making process or in working on the implementation of initiatives. They bring new facts, insights, and recommendations that can enlighten clients and challenge their preconceived views. These studies can be good input to a 24/7 effort—if the client can afford the time to wait for their completion.

## OD/HR Consulting

This type of consulting specializes in organization development (OD) and human resources (HR), addressing such issues as change management, organization design, compensation, training, and workforce motivation. Occasionally OD/HR consulting is applied to strategy (Freedman, Zackrison, and Freedman, 2001). Many OD/HR consultants work as internal consultants in large businesses and sometimes do strategy work in those firms (Scott, 2000). A majority of their projects are tactical, like team building, redesigning structures and reward systems, and conducting training programs.

When doing actual strategy work, OD/HR consulting relies on brief retreats and exercises to help clients in discussing and visioning a new strategy. These exercises are designed to elicit an inspiring, preferred vision for the company (Sheila, 2007; Waltzer, 1996). OD/HR consultants emphasize identifying the firm's strengths through questions like, "What do we do well?" combined with future-oriented questions like, "What should the organization look like in five years?" The language and concepts are largely behavioral and organizational, not usually about competitors, markets, and economics. Their clients tend to be public and nonprofit organizations.

OD/HR consulting is more real time than conventional strategy consulting because it involves organization members directly from the outset. OD/HR consulting assumes, as we do, that strategy resides in members' heads and hearts, and the key challenge is to unleash it through shared inquiry and social dialogue (Lipton, 2003). When members own the strategy, they are committed to executing it (Schein and Gallos, 2006). Here is an example from an OD/HR consulting firm in the United Kingdom:

> We don't even believe in providing our clients with definitive answers. Rather, we prefer to show their people how to come up with the right solution themselves—by applying the power of

their own intuition. That way they really believe in the strategy. And they won't let anything get in the way of its execution. Then things start to happen. And one small success inspires an even bigger one.

Unlike our approach, most OD/HR consulting projects proceed with little in-depth attention to the external marketplace and the use of economic language; little analysis is done on competitors and the position of the firm in its industry. OD/HR consulting sticks closely to its subject matter expertise of behavioral issues. It teaches managers to envision a new and successful strategy in a projective and idealistic way without being preoccupied with competitors or their products, similar to the message in *Blue Ocean Strategy* (Kim and Mauborgne, 2005).

## Strategy Facilitation

*Strategy facilitation* combines the best of the conventional and OD/HR approaches while correcting for their deficiencies. It encompasses the economic and marketing content of conventional consulting plus the behavioral and organizational processes of OD/HR consulting (Beer and Nohria, 2000). *Dynamic strategy-making* also uses guided involvement to produce a statement of strategic direction, and thereby a strategic system to guide employee behavior. We have explained and described this facilitative form of strategy consulting in Chapters Four through Seven.

Strategy facilitation provides not only an organized context but a set of tools, including the 4D framework, for managers to use in their situational assessment, as well as the four key elements for recording their conclusions on the strategic statement. It also leaves the client with the necessary learning for how to do real-time strategy in the future without outside help.

Because strategy-making addresses both content and process issues, strategy facilitation is not easily performed by one person.

It may require that two strategy facilitators work together, preferably one of them being highly experienced and knowledgeable about strategic content and the other about process and change management. They begin by contracting with senior executives, explaining how they work and what is expected of both parties. It is essential to build a strong working relationship with the CEO and members of the top team early in the process.

Strategy facilitators initially work with the CEO to plan and organize a series of off-site retreats where the discussion is aimed at building a dynamic strategic system on which the content can be added or removed as events change over time. (Much of how strategy facilitation works at the retreats and soon afterward is covered in Chapter Seven on guided involvement.) Retreats must be organized around strategic content, with the objective of helping participants discover new market opportunities and match them against the firm's capabilities. Strategy facilitators should obviously not force their views on management; rather, their job is to provide the context for stimulating and drawing useful ideas and opinions from managers and move them more to consensus.

Consultants who do strategy facilitation must possess knowledge and skills from five disciplines: corporate strategy, economics, marketing, organization, and psychology. Facilitators can't be experts on all five, but they must not be wedded to any single discipline, and they must be able to integrate across the five for clients. In addition, they must be familiar with useful analytical frameworks for making a strategic assessment. Strategy facilitators must be experienced and good at using guided involvement in off-site retreats and be sensitive to when to push the top team and when to back off. They must also be capable of getting the team to put its conclusions in writing and helping to produce a clear, concise strategic statement.

Strategy facilitators need special process expertise and credibility. They must not only be knowledgeable about how to integrate strategy content with real-time processes but be capable of questioning and confronting entrenched opinions among senior executives. They must appear creditable, possessing a success-ful track record in working with organizations on strategic issues.

These skills and knowledge are probably best learned through experience in working with firms on applied problem solving. Strategic content can be picked up in a business school where all of the relevant disciplines are covered. Behavioral and consulting skills can be learned at workshops, skill-building exercises, and schools that emphasize OD skills, such as Case Western Reserve University, Benedictine University, and the Fielding Graduate University. There are many good books and articles available on strategic content, organization development, human resource management, process facilitation, and management consulting. The challenge in reading them is to look for how they can be integrated and made understandable for clients.

Strategy facilitation is still in its infancy, and much needs to be learned about how it should be done and the skills and knowledge required to do it well. Based on our experience, we offer a few cautionary speculations.

## Clients Beware: Choosing and Managing Consultants

Organizations face a challenge in finding, selecting, and managing strategy facilitators. Make the wrong decision, and a conventional or OD/HR consultant will show up. Consultants tend to look alike, wear suits and ties, carry briefcases, make good presentations, and possess good résumés with lots of references based on extensive consulting experience. And if that is not confusing enough, they usually work in one of four types of consulting firms that all look alike but use different in-house approaches to work with clients, reflecting their firm's cultures and the kind of employees they hire:

- *Mental adventurers.* These firms employ many Ph.D.s to study broad market and social issues and predict future events, like the future of the champagne market a decade off. They are mainly conventional strategy consultants, preferring quantitative studies over qualitative, and although they give recommendations, they aren't especially interested in hanging around for implementation.

- *Strategic navigators.* These are the conventional strategy consultants focused on markets and economics, using data and analytical models to study a client's strategy problem. They mainly look outside the firm at the market and analyze the issues with economic, marketing, and finance frameworks. They like to formulate strategy and recommendations, believing that the client is responsible for execution.

- *Management physicians.* Some firms look not only at the market but inside the firm for the root cause of strategic problems, such as a lack of leadership and a poorly designed organization. They rely a lot on interviews and are concerned with implementation. They do conventional strategy work but also have behavioral and strategy facilitators. They may be lacking in focus on external issues of strategy content and the competition aspects.

- *System architects.* These firms are mainly concerned with tactical strategic issues, like the use of information systems to gain competitive advantage and cost reduction. They examine the value chain, install new systems, and arrange outsourcing for clients. They are very hands-on, but sometimes they get lost in the trees absent a broader perspective.

It is easy to be misled by consultants from these four types of firms—all of which say they do strategy. Clients must inquire more deeply to discover what's behind their sales pitch, especially if they want a strategy facilitator. Those making the selection should include not only the CEO but representatives of the board and senior management. They must inquire about the methods and approaches of the consultant and search for differences by asking good questions, such as: "What is your experience and knowledge in combining strategy content with involvement methods, and how do you achieve it?" Here are other questions to ask when inquiring if they can provide 24/7 help:

- How much do you try to identify opportunities in the market where we can use our internal strengths to exploit? Strategy facilitators have this broader and integrative perspective.

- How much will you involve us during the project— intensively from the outset or periodically for feedback sessions? Strategy facilitators use involvement throughout.

- How much do you rely on us for insight and opinions? Strategy facilitators rely on the knowledge and experience of those participating.

- Do you supply us with understandable frameworks to help us analyze and record conclusions? What are these frameworks? Strategy facilitators provide useful frameworks to help with analysis and record conclusions.

- Will you stick around to help us follow up and implement? Strategy facilitators give assistance on execution from the outset.

The answers to these questions by consultants may contain a lot of PR spin, so one should probe for specifics (Lewis, 2004). Selecting an internal consultant as a strategy facilitator is easier because they are known within the organization. Important here is to assess the record of internal consultants for standing up to management in confronting difficult issues; this is a challenging role for them to play because their jobs may depend on what they say (Scott, 2000).

Real-time strategy facilitators must move fast, and it is up to clients to keep up with and manage them. A good back-and-forth relationship and frequent discussions will ensure good results. This happened at Petrofuels between Wil Martin, the CEO, and the two strategy facilitators. The following guides can help organizations effectively manage strategy facilitators:

- Make sure that the consultants interview all those coming to a workshop; this helps to build a future relationship of openness and trust.
- Share control with the consultants, but end the relationship if you feel uncomfortable.
- Discuss each intervention so that you understand it, and make suggestions. Ask lots of questions about what is about to happen.
- Be ready to make interventions yourself to advance the process. The consultant can't do everything; ask what you can do. Give logistical support to the facilitators.

Several books about consulting can be helpful. A good book on the consulting process is Block's *Flawless Consulting* (1999). A broader perspective about the current consulting landscape is *The Contemporary Consultant* (Greiner and Poulfelt, 2005). And one on selecting consultants is *Choosing and Using Consultants and Advisors: A Best Practice Guide to Making the Right Decisions and Getting Good Value* (Lewis, 2004). And on facilitation, see *The Skilled Facilitator Fieldbook: Tips, Tools, and Tested Methods for Consultants, Facilitators, Managers, Trainers, and Coaches* (Schwarz, Davidson, Carlson, and McKinney, 2005).

## Bumps from Experience

We have encountered some bumps on the road in doing strategy facilitation, and want to pass on that learning. Sometimes we came up short as we experimented with different designs for the strategic statement and the structure of retreats. Other times we have said no when we felt uncomfortable about our relationship with the CEO or the organization. To walk away is not easy for consultants. Here are some hard-learned lessons:

- *Don't do stuff the client should do.* In the beginning, we tried to write the strategic statement for the senior team, and members didn't like the way we prepared it. From then on, we asked the team to write its own statements. Strategy facilitators should resist taking over activities that incorporate local knowledge.

- *Make sure you are working with the right kind of CEO.* We had a CEO client who insisted on her content dominating the top team's discussion. We didn't adjust or push back, and the process ended with little productive debate or commitment to a new direction. Facilitators should assess early in the process whether the CEO's style is likely to promote participation or thwart member social dialogue. In situations where the CEO is intimidating and good participation is unlikely, facilitators would be wise to seek another client. We have increasingly come to the conclusion that the top leader's behavior can build or destroy strategy-making. Proceeding with the wrong CEO can waste a lot of time.

- *Be certain that turnover in CEO and management team won't come soon.* About halfway through one of our strategy projects, the CEO and a few key team members abruptly left the company, bringing everything to a swift end. We had failed to check at the start about the likely longevity of key members. Had we probed more deeply, we might have discovered the long-simmering conflict between the CEO and the chairman of the board who founded the firm and did not want anyone messing with his baby. We had never met the chairman and thus did not discuss the project with him or learn his views about the firm. We should have.

- *Always get involved with the follow-up.* Early on, we worked with clients who wanted our help only to create a strategic statement. Once this was accomplished, we moved on. This turned out to be a mistake because implementation was spotty. Creating a statement is generally much easier than turning it into reality. While follow-up and execution are the responsibility of the top team, they likely need advice on how to organize and make this happen.

- *Know your limits.* The CEO can make interventions that the facilitator cannot—as Wil Martin did by taking a walk with Jack Davis. We were tempted to intervene when Martin adjourned the meeting and set off with Jack. If you are a control freak, watch out. Consultants must recognize their limits.

## Future for Strategy Facilitation

Since the 24/7 world is growing in its real-time demands, both conventional and OD/HR consultants increasingly will be asked by clients to act as strategy facilitators. In response to rising requests, the pressure will be on schools to train more students in strategy facilitation. Similarly, conventional and OD/HR consulting firms will be pressed to either hire strategy facilitators or retrain consultants to act as facilitators. Organizations with internal consultants and existing CSOs will need to ask them to improve their skills in a 24/7 direction of strategy implementation. The more that organizations build these skills in-house, the better prepared they will be to do real-time strategy-making on their own in the future.

Conventional strategy consultants probably already have most strategy content skills; some may be overly attached to a single discipline but can work with others who have the complementary knowledge. Some already have experience working with clients but need to learn real-time alternatives, such as e-mail interviews, to the lengthy data-gathering studies they are accustomed to doing. They will also need to learn how to facilitate a high-involvement strategy-making process. They may find strategy facilitators already in their firms with whom they can work and learn. They may attend occasional seminars on how to run effective workshops and facilitate productive social dialogue.

OD/HR consultants already have most of the skills for involving groups in problem solving, but they need to acquire strategy content knowledge and learn how to integrate it with the behavioral and organizational issues they are used to dealing with. Short of getting a business degree, we recommend taking a local course in corporate strategy, reading the literature cited in Chapter Three, and absorbing the lessons we have distilled. They also will have to let go of their attachment to favorite interventions such as team building and vision setting, and learn how to build teams while working on the content of strategy. Knowing how to run a retreat like the ones described in Chapters Six and Seven is essential.

We are not interested in selling ourselves as strategy facilitators; far from it. But we want to spread the word about *dynamic strategy-making* and its requirements. We hope this book will increase the supply and demand for strategy facilitators, as well as enhance appreciation by senior executives for real-time strategy-making. Many consulting firms already employ strategy facilitators who can teach and work with other colleagues. Client organizations have to become knowledgeable about real-time strategy-making. Once clients establish a living strategic system through the help of strategy facilitators, they should be able to maintain and sustain it by themselves.

# 10

# REAL-TIME ISSUES FAQ

We have applied *dynamic strategy-making* in a variety of organizations, from small to large and across many industries. Invariably questions arise about its applicability to different issues and contexts. In this chapter, we address some of the questions we most often hear.

## How Can We Get Slow-Moving, Tradition-Bound Firms Going on Real-Time Strategy-Making?

Many executives who are long accustomed to bureaucratic planning cycles must have the courage and initiative to begin real-time strategy-making. For them, the train has left the station; today is tomorrow. Traditional planning practices have been outdated by a fast-moving world that requires more dynamic approaches, like those examined in this book.

Many managements are unable to break free of their ritualistic addiction to traditional planning methods geared to calendars, budgets, and capital spending. Someone needs to step forward to say, "Let's begin real-time strategic planning." Since rocking the boat has not been a norm in these organizations, these typical responses will come back: "We are already doing well" and "Our current strategy is working, and the method is fine." Unfortunately, reactions that advocate the same old status quo practices were, for example, the response at GM in judging success by truck and sports utility vehicle sales—before gas prices soared in summer 2008.

So what to do? Call in a conventional consultant? That might be the best solution to begin a study where the findings prove the naysayers wrong. Better yet, follow up this study by using a strategy facilitator who can work with the CEO and management team in discussing and building on the study's findings.

If resistance continues, the board must step in and hire a new CEO. But the selection process is critical to choose a leader with a comprehensive mind-set toward strategy and a collaborative behavioral style, as described in Chapter Eight. That person should also be aware of real-time planning approaches.

In all of this, CEOs and senior managers should not defer to the past and to experts; they need to step forward to lead their organizations in real-time ways to design, construct, maintain, and update their strategic systems. They must educate themselves on what goes into real-time strategy; many are not aware of what this involves. The same admonition applies to staff planning groups responsible for giving assistance. All of these internal parties must exercise initiative in rejecting conventional ways of doing formal strategic planning.

## What Should We Do When There Is Turnover in the CEO Position and Top Team, with Implications for Lack of Continuity in an Ongoing Real-Time System?

Passing the baton is important because CEOs are indeed chief strategy officers. It is a mistake to automatically select the next in line to be chief executive. CEO tenure currently averages five years, which means lack of continuity and problems of succession. There is no honeymoon period for new CEOs: the pressure is on in public companies for immediate results. This greatly reduces the time available for CEOs to initiate and lead a dynamic process of strategy-making.

Let's take the situation where a firm already has a real-time strategic system. When the CEO exits here, there can be transition problems. It is much easier to name an insider CEO who is used to the system and wants to continue it. But transition can be problematic if the new CEO is an outsider; research has shown that outsider CEOs make more changes and bring in more new lieutenants, as happened at Coast Yellow Pages, where the outsiders presided over strategic failure. Here the board may play a key role by resisting the temptation to go outside unless they can find someone who knows about real-time planning and has the leadership characteristics noted in Chapter Eight. At Petrofuels Energy, Wil Martin was such a person coming from outside.

Additional caution must be exercised when the organization is not using real-time methods, and the board wants to make a shift to more *dynamic strategy-making*. The best bet here is an "inside outsider," like Jack Welch, who is capable but detached from past practices, according to Bower (2007).

## How Can We Involve the Board in Strategy-Making?

For too long, boards of directors have been left out of the strategy equation except for giving formal approval after the fact (Nadler, Behan, and Nadler, 2006). Now all that is changing. Sarbanes-Oxley is pressing for increased transparency and demanding greater involvement by boards of directors in strategic planning and the oversight of strategy. According to a recent McKinsey survey (2008), the results attest to growing board involvement in not only approval but in challenging the strategy of the firm. Unfortunately, many board members have been conditioned by traditional strategic planning approaches, so they have to be circumspect as they proceed. Not only do they need to evaluate the strategy of their firms, but more important, ascertain that the planning practices are in-tune with real-time realities. They should update and inform themselves about the real-time design of strategic systems and provide more oversight of strategy-making in the organization. And there are further steps among these responsibilities that they can take:

- Selecting CEOs with the experience, desired personality, and style to run a real-time strategic system and organization

- Creating a standing committee on strategy and appointing board members to it with an appreciation for real-time approaches
- Including board representatives from the standing committee to involve themselves and work with management as they engage in strategy-making and give frequent reports to the board
- Giving support to the CEO when strategic changes have to be made to real-time methods
- Ensuring continuous follow-up and continuity by management to reinforce *dynamic strategy-making*

The board must restrain itself at times. It cannot set the strategy for the firm because many members are not executives responsible for executing it. We have consulted to clients where board members participated with the senior management team in their strategy sessions, and they made valuable contributions that reflected the thoughts of the board.

## Can Real-Time Strategy-Making Be Used in Organizations Operating in Countries and Regions Outside North America?

So far our experience, with a few exceptions, has been with real-time strategy-making primarily in North America and the West, where the culture is fairly compatible with high-involvement methods and explicitly written statements. Managers from North America and Europe have long held values supporting individualism, open participation, speaking up, and that words in writing mean what they say. Consequently organizations populated with these managers are likely to favor methods that promote individual involvement and explicit written communication, such as the real-time methods described here.

Problems can arise, however, when Western values of individualism run head on into the organizational culture needed for social dialogue and team decision making. In doing strategy facilitation, we often experience an underlying tension between the power of the group and the power of the individual; Latin American, Eastern Europe, and India, for example, strongly believe that there should be power differences among people. Organizations operating in these countries are likely to have problems with involving members in team strategy-making.

Our experience in applying 24/7 methods at two large Mexican companies suggests that the process may have to be adjusted to fit cultural values. Here, real-time strategy-making was more formal and top down than in North America; it was more autocratic and hierarchically driven. This required us to intervene more forcefully to surface participants' disagreements, solicit their opinions, and encourage them to share ideas; they were hesitant to speak up and challenge viewpoints, especially when they came from those higher up in the organization.

In Asia, cultural values promote social cohesion, avoidance of uncertainty, and indirect communication where the context gives more meaning than the words. Although Asian firms would likely favor the group dynamics in real-time strategy-making, they would probably have trouble dealing with its uncertainty and clear written outcomes. We have lectured about real-time methods in Asia and find managers interested in them. Our single experience in doing real-time strategy-making with an entrepreneurial firm founded and run by Asian executives underscores these difficulties. They were reluctant to engage in any kind of strategy activities until the owner, "Chairman Ma," approved. We had to push them to address the uncertainties inherent in their fast-paced market; they didn't want to write things down for fear the words would be "misinterpreted by Chairman Ma."

## Do 24/7 Methods Apply to Nonprofit and Government Organizations?

Both nonprofits and public organizations need a real-time strategy because many face fast-moving events. We have applied the same thinking and methodology to several nonprofit clients, including a major academic organization with eighteen thousand members, a large college of liberal arts and sciences, a theater school of a major university, and the board of another academic association involved in executive education.

All of these organizations have competitors: for donors, students, and employees. Public organizations also have customers for whom they provide a service. Many public organizations are being deregulated and privatized. For example, school systems are faced with the growth of charter schools, many of which have been more successful relative to public schools.

Working with nonprofits requires that facilitators eliminate such words as *profit, business,* and *sales* from their vocabulary. However, we remind the leaders of these organizations that they indeed have customers to attract and serve and that they are competing against other nonprofits for funds and volunteers. Potential customers are evaluating what the nonprofit or public organization has to offer versus other choices. Nonprofits don't have profits as a bottom line, but most have budgets with revenues and expenses; they need increased revenues for growth and improved services. Many nonprofits are also staffed with unpaid volunteers who come and go as they wish; a high-involvement strategic system that includes their common cause can provide the needed glue to attract and hold employees together.

It is easy to convince leaders of these organizations with these arguments. Then they are able to draft strategic statements with all four elements covered. As an example, at one university, a college of liberal arts and sciences with a group of thirty-two department chairs concluded that to become more competitive, the college would have to recruit big-name professors to certain departments where they were already strong. But to do so, the college would need to add $100 million to its endowment for chairs—which it proceeded to do. Through considerable debate and open dialogue, the dean and department chairs were able to support this strategy and went on to achieve it.

## How Can We Gauge Whether an Organization Is Incompatible with 24/7 Methods and Therefore Should Not Embark on it?

Managers need to know when not to engage in real-time strategy-making. Although we have tried to build a case for *dynamic strategy-making*, there are some organizations and situations that should probably avoid it. The first ones that come to mind are organizations facing an immediate crisis that needs to be resolved before strategy-making can be contemplated. At Petrofuels, the budget deficit required urgent attention and resolution before the top team could focus on strategy.

Another organization that should refrain from creating a *dynamic strategy-making* approach is the one with a CEO who is not respected or whose top group is not really a team, as at Gamma Bank. The CEO may not match the personality profile in Chapter Eight or the team may soon change in its composition. Also, a CEO and team must want to engage in the process. If they lack desire, the approach will not work.

Caution is advised also when a resistant board has different ideas about strategy-making, as happened at Coast Yellow Pages. However, board members can be won over by including them in the strategy process.

In addition, if some major event is pending, such as a strike or a public offering, postpone *dynamic strategy-making* until that event is behind you. Finally, if the organization is not used to change, there may have to be preparatory work to create a sense of urgency.

## How Can Approaches to Strategy Like *Dynamic Strategy-Making* Be Improved?

Real-time approaches to strategy can be made more effective by fine-tuning the existing approach or coming up with new concepts and methods. This book has presented one approach, but as we have said, it will improve with further application and feedback. In this direction, there are implications, some of them profound, for both scholars and consultants.

Scholars have avoided the dirty, hands-on practical side of strategy-making for too long; instead, they have preferred to focus on impersonal data gathering and theory development rather than getting involved, as if that step might bias their work and they might be accused of selling out for added income. Although we continue to need theory building and findings in developing and checking out and validating strategic theories, we also need scholarly work in the trenches (Van de Ven, 1992). Academics, especially those in business schools, should be concerned with helping managers and organizations form and execute their strategies in a real-time mode, so that their enterprises are not overwhelmed by accelerating events around them.

Scholars can still wear their research hats if they accept the notion that strategy is no longer a separate topic to be studied apart from its context. Research is critical to determine what leads to what results as leaders engage in traditional and real-time strategy making. Evaluative research can yield important findings about the role of the CEO and top team as they engage in strategy-making. Also we need more knowledge about various kinds of interventions relevant today, such as how to hold large mass meetings that not only inform but inspire the workforce.

Scholars are ideally suited to the 24/7 world because they can operate as facilitators without the pressure of making lengthy studies to cover overhead costs. In this role, one can learn as well as make contributions. Access to management has always been a problem for scholars, but getting involved as a facilitator provides an opening for research. We write down everything that happens; the cases in the appendixes are examples. We have continued to write scholarly publications from our experience. Care should be taken here to avoid biased findings; we recommend having a collaborator along to be a good check on biases. A side benefit for scholars is they can bring their real-world experience and knowledge into the classroom as a way of training future managers.

Full-time consultants can provide vital help to scholars and benefit themselves. They are out on the firing line and can develop and share their approaches. They too can become strategy facilitators, even if they are conventional strategy consultants; 24/7 approaches can begin with presenting findings from conventional strategy studies at a retreat like those described in this book. Consultants can also invent new dynamic methods to speed up the process of formulating, implementing, and revising a strategy. Needed too are innovative approaches to permeate the organization with ways to embrace the workforce in getting them on board and "behaving the strategies."

Consultants can also invite scholars to work with them. For too long, both parties have gone their separate ways, even though they became acquainted in business school. They can go back to their favorite strategy teacher and jointly author cases and articles. The role of the scholar-consultant needs to become more accepted in both consulting firms and in academe.

## New Mind-Set

There are obviously other questions, such as issues of companies going green and winning over unions, but we trust that readers with this new mind-set can see how these issues can be resolved by a system that allows tailoring content and process to the situation. Chapter Eleven summarizes the main themes underlying this book with some last words on them. These themes must become the strategic mind-set of all people involved—scholars, consultants, and managers—in seeing *dynamic strategy-making* through to success.

# 11

# LAST WORDS ON UNDERLYING THEMES

*Dynamic strategy-making* is a way of thinking, a new mind-set, about forming, executing, revising, and leading strategy in today's fast-paced world. In writing this book, we have tried to convey what we have learned about real-time strategy-making from our own consulting experience, research, and the strategy literature. We have organized and shared this learning here, and we hope it is useful to leaders, consultants, and scholars doing strategy-making and students in the subject. Our ideas and methods are not intended to be another popular management technique or elixir for strategic success. Rather, they represent a particular stance or attitude toward strategy-making within an ever changing context.

We believe our approach is unique in offering several original contributions centered around the introduction of a strategic system that permeates the organization and is renewable while creating competitive advantage in a 24/7 world. Within this overall framework there are other specific contributions: (1) providing the 4D framework for assessment, (2) crafting a statement of strategic direction, and (3) using guided involvement as a process to stimulate this content, (4) all aided by the support of strategy facilitation.

We do not expect readers to agree with all of our views and prescriptions. Healthy skepticism and questioning are essential to good leadership and strategy development. Running through the book are some underlying messages about real-time strategy-making that we believe are worth highlighting and pondering. We conclude by summarizing these fundamental themes.

## Strategy-Making Is a Dynamic Process

Real-time strategy-making is a dynamic process that keeps organizations competitive in the face of changing conditions. This action orientation means that strategy-making is proactive and forward looking, not passive and reactionary. Firms need to consider new sources of competitive advantage and new market opportunities well before they are apparent to competitors. Then they must take the necessary actions today to ensure that those favorable conditions actually happen in their organizations. Real-time strategy-making is also ongoing and changing, not a periodic or one-time static event. Organizations constantly assess and make requisite changes in their strategies. They examine themselves and their environment looking for better ways to exploit their capabilities and explore for new prospects. They must adjust strategic content to keep pace with relevant environmental changes. They keep the organization aligned with strategic direction.

The pace or timing of these ongoing activities varies depending on the rate at which the competitive environment is changing. In some companies, for example, strategy-making moves gradually for long periods, yet accelerates rapidly when conditions change abruptly, such as happened at IBM in the 1990s. U.S. steelmaking also moved slowly until new automated technology and overseas competitors produced a revolution. In some industries, such as biotechnology and entertainment, strategy-making must be fast paced to keep up with the competitive environment.

## Strategy-Making Is a Human and Social Process

At its core, strategy-making is a human and social process carried out by people in the context of interaction with others. It is easy to lose sight of this simple reality and get caught up in the business and analytical aspects of strategy-making. Organizations that neglect this side do so at their peril. Because people, and the teams they comprise, are the instruments for making strategy, success is heavily influenced by the talents and foibles that members and teams bring with them to the process.

Capable strategic leadership like that described in Chapter Eight can go a long way in moving organizations forward in the right strategic direction. A top team with competent members and norms supporting open dialogue and active listening can create innovative strategies that members could not do acting alone. Conversely, participants' cognitive biases, such as overoptimism and loss aversion, can adversely affect strategic decisions (Kahneman and Tversky, 1979). Teams can also fall prey to decision-making problems, such as groupthink (Janis, 1982) and "risky shift" (Myers and Bishop, 1970). These personal biases and group problems are most likely to occur in situations that are highly complex and uncertain—exactly the conditions encountered in real-time strategy-making.

Fortunately, there are effective methods for helping members confront and resolve these issues. We have described some of them in the chapters on guided involvement and the strategy facilitator, and there are plenty of other methods available (see, for example, Robins, 2004, and Schein, 1998). The key is to treat the social and human side of strategy-making as essential to success. This means taking full advantage of the special talents that humans bring to strategy-making by creating the conditions that support and enable them to participate and become involved. It means keeping an active vigil on how things are progressing and making timely and relevant interventions when needed.

## Strategy-Making Is a Learning Process

Strategy-making is a learning process in which members must find out how to create, execute, and revise strategy. They must learn about the organization and its competitive environment so they can make informed choices about strategic content. They must learn how to enact the strategy, translating strategic content into actions and behaviors necessary to make it happen. Members must learn how to revise strategy as things change. They must learn how to improve the strategy-making process itself. In fast-paced environments, such learning is essential for organization success. The faster and more effectively organizations can learn, the more quickly and better they will respond to change.

Regrettably, organizations tend not to appreciate the magnitude and kind of learning involved in strategy-making. A new strategy generally requires significant changes in behavior—for example, how members perform tasks and interact with each other and customers.

Behavioral change cannot take place through abstract or passive means. Rather, people can learn new behavior only through behaving—trying to do it, observing the consequences, making adjustments, and so on (Argyris, 1999). This action learning is the core of strategy execution and needs to occur at multiple levels throughout the organization: individuals learning new work tasks, teams learning new interaction patterns, and multiple units learning how to coordinate their efforts.

Most organizations are not designed to support action learning, which requires safe experimentation, careful analysis of the results, and reflective sharing of what is learned. Worse yet, organizations are full of barriers that actively impede learning: management practices that punish failed experiments and those doing them, information and reward systems that reinforce routines and habits, and structures that hinder sharing knowledge and experience across the organization (Snyder and Cummings, 1998).

At a higher level, organizations need to attend to the kind of learning for improving the strategy-making process while taking account of how well they are doing in strategy-making and how to improve it. This second-order learning helps organizations learn how to learn. In assessing and seeking to improve the learning needed for strategy-making, members add to the organization's capacity to learn. This is no small achievement. Organization learning capability is difficult to develop or acquire, so it can be a valuable source of sustained competitive advantage. In today's marketplace, it may be what separates winning strategy-makers from failures.

## Strategy-Making Is a Situational Process

In strategy-making, the situation matters. The process takes place in a particular organizational context with unique features, dynamics, and demands. Organizations must account for these differences in deciding how to do strategy-making; they cannot simply adopt a generic method or a technique that has worked elsewhere and expect it to work in their situation.

We think the methods and frameworks we have described in this book are geared to recognizing the uniqueness of each situation and incorporating data about it. The methods are flexible and open to including strategic content by involving executives who make their own assessments and conclusions about their situation. These leaders are also responsible for implementing and monitoring the strategic system and extending openness out to the highly involved workforce—all aware that their feedback makes a difference.

But we do not mean to suggest that the approach outlined here is the answer. Far from it. We have been experimenting for years with the development of what we call *dynamic strategy-making*, and we will continue to do so. Every organization needs to develop its own way of dealing with a fast-paced world. We have offered one approach for launching and leading real-time strategy-making that we believe can be successfully adapted to particular organizations.

Our model and methods should not be regarded as the only approach, nor should it be applied like a cookie cutter to manipulate the firm into a given method. Each organization should tailor its own approach to strategy-making to fit its situation. It might start from scratch or with an established approach and then adjust and modify it as the situation demands. In all of the organizations with which we have worked, we have helped participants tailor the strategy-making process as it proceeded. This helped them build and take ownership for their own approach to strategy-making—one they could commit to and make work for them.

In today's fast-paced world, organizations cannot go too far astray so long as they approach strategy-making from a dynamic perspective. They need to create a real-time strategy-making process that is forward looking and constantly changing: a process driven by strategic leaders that is highly involving and accounts for participants' human and social strengths and flaws; a process that supports and enables the kinds of learning needed to assess the organization and its environment, change members' behaviors, and improve strategy-making; and a process tailored to fit the firm's unique situation so it becomes part of organizational life. We hope *Dynamic Strategy-Making* has stimulated this kind of thinking and action.

# Appendix A

## COAST YELLOW PAGES – A RESEARCH CASE STUDY

The Senior Management Group (SMG) of Coast Yellow Pages (CYP) had recently called for a postmortem of the Metro Rescope project. Described as a $75 million gamble, the project had reconfigured yellow pages directories in CYP's largest market, the Metro Basin, to defend its eroding market share. It introduced five new community yellow pages directories based on changing shopping patterns while retaining the big Metro white pages.

The Metro Rescope was the first major project for CYP under the new CEO, Jack Anderson. During its implementation in the past year, the Metro Rescope sales campaign was characterized by periods of turmoil and virtual work stoppage by the sales force at critical times with complaints about wages and targets. Although Rescope had been a major change given CYP's historical context, Anderson believed the company will face several more radical innovations in the near future. The SMG wanted to know what the company could learn from the Metro Rescope experience that would help manage the critical issues ahead.

CYP is a stand-alone subsidiary of Western Telephone with the objective of becoming a technological and market leader in the reference information industry. Its products at the time of its formation were the white and yellow page directories for the geographical regions served by Western Telephone. CYP's parent expected it to place a strong emphasis on business development and growth.

A senior executive described the historical relationship between Western and CYP as follows: "Historically, few at

Telephone have really understood how the business works except that it makes a lot of money. After prices were deregulated, they've been raising advertising prices year after year almost at will." CYP is treated as a classic cash cow with a lot of pressure on it to generate high net income.

After deregulation and Bell divestiture, the industry structure became fragmented, with ten major players, including former AT&T companies, non-Bell affiliated telephone companies, and former contract sales agents that had begun to transform themselves into integrated yellow pages publishers. During this period of deregulation, other media were also gaining visibility as potential alternatives, especially for advertisers seeking to move from mass to targeted marketing. The best-known examples were teletext, videotext, and electronic yellow pages; national classified advertising services; talking yellow pages; and national electronic yellow pages.

CYP, with its heritage as a department of Western Telephone, had inherited the culture of the 100,000-employee regulated monopoly. Furthermore, CYP was historically not viewed as part of the mainstream of providing telephone service in the Western Telephone system and therefore operated out of the limelight. As a result, people who were transferred to CYP tended to remain there, and the culture became inbred over time. A Western Telephone veteran who recently joined CYP described it this way: "Yellow Pages was treated as a stepchild of the telephone company.... When I came into CYP, I felt I was entering a company that had been hiding behind the doors of change for fifteen years. It was like the telephone company fifteen years ago with hostility, fear of outsiders, and resistance toward change."

Several executives described the old organization as "mechanistically run." It was organized into functional units with prescribed policies and procedures. Managers "did not cross functional boundaries to get things done." The system was also labor intensive. Of CYP's 2,400 employees, 870 worked in paper processing activities related to contract management, listings management, and prepress activities. One senior executive who joined CYP prepared a list, after one week on the job, of organizational characteristics that stood out in the company:

- People don't talk about or think about profitability.
- People focus on their own suborganization rather than the total company.
- There is a blind "forward-march" mentality and no thinking about planning and long-term direction.
- Process seems more important than results, with a lot of time spent in meetings.
- There appears to be a negative predisposition. Company rumors, for example, are all negative.

## Recent Management Changes at CYP

The new CEO, Jack Anderson, had been senior vice president and managing partner of an international general management consulting firm before joining the Western Telephone Group as vice president of corporate strategy and development. In his role as corporate strategist, he had prepared a long-term vision statement and strategic plan for the Western Telephone Group. Anderson recalled his strategic priorities when he came to CYP:

> Many of us in corporate strategy believed that CYP was seriously underdeveloped as a business, that there were many elements of the existing business that needed focus and attention. Similarly, the CYP business in general had great potential to expand into areas that utilized its sales and marketing channels, and leveraged the enormously powerful western states business economy. My first priority was to focus on the parts of the business that most urgently needed repair, and to attract a team of managers that could get it done. Beyond that, it was time to build a future for the company.

Other changes at the top included a new vice president and chief financial officer and a new vice president of marketing and business development. These four executives formed CYP's top management team. In addition, three of the seven sales and marketing vice presidents to the CEO were either replaced or retired, as were seven of ten sales branch managers.

The sales force consisted of approximately eight hundred unionized telephone and premise sales representatives organized around branches in major cities. Sales contacts with existing and potential advertisers were made as part of the annual campaign—a concentrated period during which sales reps systematically covered a specific region. Before the start of a campaign, the yellow pages system generated "equitable" assignments for each sales rep assigned to a campaign. To ensure equitable allocation of advertising revenue to the different reps, the system was set up to shuffle around advertiser accounts each year. In any year, therefore, 80 percent of a sales rep's assigned contacts were "new" contacts.

The sales force had a culture that was unique within CYP. A manager described its origins:

> Years ago the company looked at the need to publish yellow pages and asked, "How do we move the sales force around the states on a publishing cycle that won't have peaks and valleys to it?" So a process was set up that required a nomad sales force that moved from place to place and sold yellow page advertisements in little towns. As a result, we ended up with people that had no homes and lived in trailer parks and motels. They are still free souls. They cling to the concept of being road warriors, macho, lovers, pirates, and take pride in being rabble rousers.

> The sales commission structure in the company was very liberal, and sales reps made lots of money. Even the knuckle draggers would make $70,000.... They're pampered, and other people in the company see them that way. They drive Porsches; one even drove a Rolls Royce. As far as I'm concerned, money makes the world go around. I think most sales people are money motivated and look for instant gratification. Now we have people [managers] making decisions for us but relatively few of the managers have any field experience.

# Metro Rescope

Metro is the largest of CYP's markets. If the Metro market were a separate nation, its GNP, more than $100 billion, would rank nineteenth in the world. It has almost 200,000 small businesses, more than 30 percent of the western states total, and 95 percent of these businesses have fewer than fifty employees. Its 8 million residents represent the greatest buying power of any other market in the United States. The Metro market was served by twelve CYP consumer directories and one business-to-business CYP. The thirteen directories contributed 24 percent of CYP's total revenue. CYP had a 51.3 percent market share in the overall Metro Basin.

Bill Lewis, working with the vice president of sales in the Metro region, became project manager of Metro Rescope, reporting through the marketing manager to Joe Wolcott, vice president of marketing. They commissioned a market research firm to study consumer shopping habits in the Metro Basin. Their analysis indicated that the new community shopping areas of Metro region were no longer defined by municipal boundaries but spilled over traditional CYP boundaries on the basis of shopping patterns.

The Rescope idea was already in motion when Anderson joined CYP. The marketing people were committed to it because the idea made intuitive sense to everyone. However, the idea had not been subject to analytical rigor, so Anderson asked Wolcott to prepare a formal business case. The business case team was organized along the 4 P's of marketing, with key individuals assigned responsibility for product, price, place, and promotion. A fifth individual was responsible for data systems. Each of these people had two or three people in his or her area. The team worked under heavy pressure to produce a business case in four weeks. One of the team members recalled:

> Joe Wolcott wanted the business case developed immediately. The five groups plus a team of editors worked under a lot of pressure, seven days a week, to produce the business case. I think

there was a lot of form in the business case—more form than substance—just to prove to Jack Anderson that we could prepare a good looking business case.

The team had differences of opinion on several key issues, including whether the wide-area Metro yellow pages CYP ought to be eliminated or whether smaller community directories ought to be superimposed on the existing CYP, thus offering advertisers more than one alternative per area. As one member described the outcome, "The team agreed to disagree, but finally, Joe Wolcott got his way on all the key issues. In this case, that meant we would offer the advertiser two directories." The business case recommended that the Metro area be rescoped according to natural boundaries.

Key business case projections were:

|  | Prior Year Revenue | Projected Revenue |
|---|---|---|
| GMAD | $41.9 million | $32.1 million + $18.4 million additional revenue from Rescope |
| Total | $41.9 million | $50.5 million |

A thirty-slide summary of the key conclusions in the business case was presented to the senior management group in March. The group approved Rescope, based on the presentation, for the Metro campaign scheduled to run from November 21 to April 24. Wolcott had the responsibility of implementing Rescope up to the point of execution.

In February and March, Wolcott employed another market research consulting firm to study advertisers about reactions to the new directories. Eight percent rated the proposed plan excellent, 29 percent good, 22 percent fair, and 33 percent poor. On the question, "Which plan do you prefer?" the executive summary stated that 25 percent preferred the proposed plan over the existing plan and an additional 12 percent had no preference.

Wolcott decided not to tell Anderson about the survey results, which were as follows:

|  | Large Advertisers | Small Advertisers |
|---|---|---|
| Prefer proposed plan | 25% | 19% |
| Prefer current plan | 63% | 70% |
| No preference | 12% | 11% |

In May, Wolcott set up a team to coordinate Rescope implementation. The team members had full-time responsibilities in other jobs and met once a week to discuss issues connected with Rescope: logistics, data systems, training, promotion, and others. Each member worked as liaison with a different part of the organization. Bill Lewis was now working in sales in Metro and was an implementation team member. Starting at the end of June, the general sales managers from Metro and surrounding areas met weekly with Lewis and Alice Davidson, then vice president of sales for the region. Karen Leskin was national branch general sales manager during this period and was involved in the meetings because the national branch sales reps had partial responsibility for Metro Rescope.

Lewis described his experience as follows:

> I would negotiate, communicate, and liaise with the sales managers on issues necessary to make Metro Rescope work in the field, and communicate back to the implementation team. It was not always pleasant because the salespeople were not very happy about it. They had not really been consulted; we had not obtained enough buy-in at the time of idea generation and development of the Rescope plan.

To obtain buy-in from key sales reps, the general sales managers formed a task force of telephone and premise sales reps for the National and Metro Rescope. The group had three meetings in August and early September. A general sales manager described them in this way:

> We were walking on eggs because we were bringing in these people to take part, but a lot of the issues had already been

decided. We had to tell them up front, "We don't get to vote about whether we're going to do it or how we're going to price it. Let's talk about how to implement it." Actually, we moved past that fairly quickly because they believed the product was good. So we talked about what would be likely objections by customers and how to overcome them.

## Compensation and Other Marketing Changes

Prior to the start of the Metro campaign in November, CYP went through several changes that would have a bearing on the campaign.

As part of the regular contract negotiations with the union, CYP's management negotiated changes in the sales compensation system. The negotiations were completed in September, thus making Metro the first major campaign under the new system. Under the old system, commissions on new accounts and increases in old accounts ranged from 70 to 200 percent of one month's billings, depending on the area. There were no penalties for loss of existing accounts except the loss of renewal commission, which was relatively low, at 8 to 17 percent of one month's billings. The old system did not link commissions to revenue goals.

Under the new system, the same commission rate applied to both renewals and new revenue. As a result, sales reps had to make up for lost accounts and show a net increase in revenue before they could earn the target commission. In addition, the new system was "objective based." For example, if management set a 28 percent increase goal in a particular campaign and it assigned a sales rep $1,000 of existing revenue, the sales rep had to return with $1,280 to earn the average target income.

In the new plan, commission rates also varied at different levels of revenue achievement. From 0 to 80 percent of total goal revenue (TGR), the commission was fairly low; between 80 and 100 percent, the rate was approximately three times that of 0 to 80 percent; and above 100 percent TGR, commission accelerated to three times the 80 to 100 percent rate. Finally, a consistency bonus was awarded if a sales rep achieved 100 percent of TGR in three campaigns during one year. Base salaries for sales reps were relatively low; in 1992, they averaged $19,000. With commissions, however, total compensation ranged from $130,000 for the top-performing premise sales rep to $38,000 for the poorest. Average compensation was $68,000 for a premise sales rep and $50,000 for a telephone sales rep.

Joe Wolcott, the marketing vice president who coordinated preparation of the Rescope business case, resigned in September 1992. His successor, Sam Cummings, joined in November and restructured marketing into business development, responsible for product and market diversification and planning; product management, responsible for enhancing the core product; and market management, consisting of a network of market managers to be stationed in the field sales offices to aid in strategy development. Metro's market manager was assigned in May 1992.

## The Metro Rescope Campaign

All Metro sales reps went through a half-day training program on the Rescope project in September. The training, done by CYP's training group, consisted of presentations on the Rescope concept and on the "how to" of paperwork and the new discount structure. A new CD product to be used with laptops showed what a customer's ad would look like. According to a sales manager, the training did not do much in terms of how to position the CD product or how to overcome customer objections to the new directories.

From September through November, Metro sales reps worked on campaigns that preceded the Metro campaign. Although the new compensation plan was introduced to the sales reps in October, it did not seem to have an immediate impact because the current campaigns operated under the old plan. In addition, a special incentive scheme had been initiated a year earlier that was scheduled to end with the close of the books preceding the Metro campaign. Under this scheme, all sales reps who bettered their previous year's performance were eligible for a trip to Hong Kong. Consequently, during the period just preceding Thanksgiving, 30 percent of the sales force traveled to Hong Kong on a holiday. The Metro campaign officially kicked off on Friday, November 21, the week before Thanksgiving. The term *kick-off* seemed a misnomer. A decade or so earlier, most campaigns closed on schedule and a new campaign started the next day with an official opening where sales managers discussed goals with the sales reps and the campaign kicked off with a lot of hoopla.

A de facto work stoppage emerged shortly after the new sales goals were announced. Sales reps were still receiving commissions from the other campaigns that had just closed, and "December seemed like a good time to take vacation." Metro was traditionally a slow starting book, as most small businesses were either too busy selling in December or were on vacation.

In January, the first commission statements under the new contract were sent out to the sales reps. A sales manager commented:

> The January commission statement was the first tangible evidence about how the sales reps were to be paid under the new system. And they were immobilized because they felt betrayed by the union and by management. Training and information about the new compensation plan had been communicated to the sales reps in October, but it had obviously not sunk in. Reality hit in January with the commission statements. They received practically no commissions. It was as if they were hearing the information for the first time. Things came to a screeching halt. Not only were the sales reps unhappy, but the sales managers were also unhappy because they were awestruck by the objective, and their compensation depended on it too.

The new compensation plan, combined with the threshold, pushed back the payment of commissions to sales reps. To meet short-term cash flow needs, the sales reps drew salary advances. By mid-January, sales reps owed five thousand to six thousand dollars each, which led to a lot of anxiety. One sales manager explained, "As a result, people just weren't selling. It wasn't an organized slowdown, but nothing was happening." The term "TGR flu" came to symbolize it, going from 69 lost days in December to 188 in February.

A sales award banquet was scheduled in Metro for January 21. The banquet was informally referred to as the "Re-kickoff" of the Metro campaign because from that date, the National Sales reps were also scheduled to start work on the campaign. A week before the banquet, Karen Leskin and her sales managers held one of their bimonthly sales force meetings. One of them described the mood:

> The environment was so thick, we couldn't walk through it any-
> more. An entourage of people were marching through Karen Leskin's
> office all the time asking, "Is there a master plan? Are you trying
> to get rid of us? We've been duped. How could all this happen?"
> Many people were hurt; many people were angry. It was obvi-
> ous we had to get past many emotional hurdles if we were to get
> anything done.

In mid-January, the CEO, Jack Anderson, heard through the grapevine that "the Metro campaign had not started yet." On January 21, he arrived late for the awards banquet. When he entered the hall, Sam Cummings was addressing the sales force on SMART, the new design concept in CYP Yellow Pages. Anderson described his reaction: "I entered and sat at the back while Sam Cummings was talking about SMART. The sales reps did not seem to be interested in what he was saying; instead they seemed to be grumbling among themselves. I was taken aback. How could the morale be so low and I didn't know about it? What was really going on?"

Anderson gave a scheduled five-minute speech to the sales force in which he made no reference to his concerns or obser-vations. The speeches were followed by cocktails during which "the sales reps were bitching," according to Anderson. "The tone of the comments was, in effect, 'I'm not going to sell your community directories; my compensation is being screwed.'"

A campaign strategy meeting was scheduled for the day after the banquet with people from marketing, sales, and the San Francisco senior management to evaluate the campaign and decide what needed to be done to get it going. This was the 40 percent point of the campaign in terms of number of days, but only 4 percent of the accounts had been serviced. During the strategy meeting, David Fleming, Karen Leskin, and Jane Hill, all members of the senior staff, committed themselves to making, before the end of that day, an action plan to "complete the Metro campaign on schedule." The plan that they prepared was a three-page document with fifteen tactical items specified, including time frames and responsibilities. Specific resources immediately committed by Ron Bower included a "lead generation group." The group became operational in mid-February and consisted of sixteen people who were scheduled to be laid off from other parts of CYP. They were assigned to Metro Sales and given the responsibility of calling advertisers, determining potential interest, and passing on leads to the sales force.

As part of the original business case, a recommendation had been made in August to hire three sales reps to address the N&D (never and don't) file, which contained fifty thousand businesses never contacted because of their low potential. After the campaign strategy meeting, action on this issue was expedited, and three sales reps were hired from competitors.

The campaign strategy group, which was in effect a crisis management task force that included Ron Bower and key managers from sales management and marketing, decided to meet every other week to evaluate progress and make decisions as the Metro campaign evolved. This decision for the group to meet every two weeks was contrary to the usual, hierarchical, bureaucratic way of doing things. The group also recommended that the compensation plan threshold level be lowered from the existing 80 percent. A week later, Bower and Anderson decided to lower the threshold level to 65 percent.

At the Metro meeting, a sales rep got up and said, "I haven't heard anything that will make me go out and sell CDs." Fleming responded, "Give me your market. I have someone who will sell your market." After a moment of silence, the sales rep sat down.

Eight new sales reps, hired from competitors, were informally called "the Hungry 8" and were given the responsibility of recanvassing. After an account was closed by a regular sales rep, a recanvasser would go back to the account and see if there was anything left to sell. The second major issue at the February meeting had to do with the Asian community in Metro. One of the Metro CDs had a high concentration of Asian businesses, and this CD also had the lowest sales rate. The Asian business community in general had been viewed as a problem in Metro because the sales force was predominantly white Caucasian and could not communicate with Asian small business proprietors. In mid-March, the three Asians brought in as interpreters were assigned to sell directly to Asian businesses.

The N&D team and the Hungry 8 received special incentive structures because they were working with low-potential accounts. The Asian reps were another special case. All Asian accounts had already been assigned to the regular reps as part of the equitable allocation process and could not be taken away. Therefore, the Asian reps were hired as managers who sold to the Asian accounts, but the commission was still earned by the regular reps. The Asian reps were motivated instead by contests and by the fact that they were temporary workers who would become permanent if they performed well. By mid-March, all three teams were up and running.

A point of emphasis made by Fleming, Leskin, and the sales managers in their interactions with the sales reps was described by a manager as follows: "If you don't go out and sell, you will guarantee yourselves that you will not make any money. The special project teams are making money from the business that you guys are turning down, so you should ask yourselves how much you could make if you went out and sold."

## April Campaign Closes

The sales force came into April with a high close rate. According to one sales manager, there seemed to have been a shift in the sales force attitude from, "If we dig in our heels, management will back down," to, "We have to go out and give it a shot."

When the campaign results were totaled, the "normal" sales force came in with a 19.8 percent increase in revenue versus about a 10 percent increase the previous year. The off-line teams had added another 5 percent, with each team exceeding objectives. The total net gain was about 24 percent, which fell short of the objective of 32 percent, but it still was greater than anything achieved in recent memory. The weekly and total Metro campaign results are in Exhibit A.1

Starting in May, the 0 to 65 percent threshold in incentives was also eliminated by the senior management group and replaced by a flat commission rate from 0 to 100 percent. This announcement was made with the entire sales force in attendance. Jack Anderson was also present. A sales rep asked, "When will we get objectives that are realistic, and when we do, will they be made retroactive?" The sales rep received a standing ovation. Anderson stood firm. He explained the purpose of the objectives and the expectations of corporate owners, and said, "I don't know whether I can change the objectives, but even if I could, I wouldn't."

## Reflections

In June, the case researchers interviewed several people for their reflections on what had happened during the Rescope experiment. Here are two of them:

> Senior manager from Metro: "Rescope was a monumental achievement."

> Senior sales manager: "The level of nonactivity in the first three months was an unpleasant surprise. We made a

## Exhibit A.1 Metro Campaign Results

## Weekly Campaign Results for Regular Metro Sales Representatives

| Period | Percentage of Objective of Regular Sales Reps |
|---|---|
| From campaign start to 1/16/92 | 3.4% |
| Week ending Jan. 23 | 4.6 |
| Week ending Jan. 30 | 13.2 |
| Week ending Feb. 6 | 18.3 |
| Week ending Feb. 13 | 22.7 |
| Week ending Feb. 20 | 26.6 |
| Week ending Feb. 27 | 32.0 |
| Week ending Mar. 6 | 38.1 |
| Week ending Mar. 13 | 43.0 |
| Week ending Mar. 20 | 49.1 |
| Week ending Mar. 27 | 53.9 |
| Week ending Apr. 3 | 58.5 |
| Week ending Apr. 10 | 63.4 |
| Week ending Apr. 17 | 68.8 |
| Week ending Apr. 24 | 75.6 |
| Week ending May 1 | 84.1 |

## Campaign Achievement by Sales Teams: Total Campaign Percentage of Objective

| Regular Metro Reps | Asian Reps | Hungry 8 Reps | N&D Reps |
|---|---|---|---|
| 84.1% | 166.0% | 95.0% | 118.0% |

## Campaign Summary (millions of dollars)

| | Rescope Case Projection | Target Revenue | Actual Revenue |
|---|---|---|---|
| Metro GMAD | $32.2 | $40.3 | $36.8 |
| CDs | $18.4 | $6.7 | $5.7 |
| Total | $50.6 | $47.0 | $42.5 |

big comeback, but the question is, Would we have done better if we had been running from the beginning?"

The CEO of CYP, Jack Anderson, reflected on the comments he had heard from his managers about Metro Rescope:

> The vision I have is to make CYP a global electronic information services company. Metro Rescope may be a major change given CYP's history, but it pales in significance when I think of what we face in the future. Most of our weaknesses were exposed in Metro—not in a planning environment where the fixes have a neat and scholarly precision: but rather in the market, where the business lives, and where minor oversights in "the plan" become nearly insurmountable crises in the execution of the business. It was a grand winner because our strengths also became very visible, and necessarily so in order to overcome the problems. We learned as a company that limits that had become part of the conventional wisdom no longer exist, and we can do things we never dreamed of. The issue now is how to build on these strengths and minimize or eliminate the problems.

One year later, Jack Anderson resigned after his parent board, which had experienced considerable turnover in its members, refused to fund his vision of creating a global electronic information company.

# Appendix B

## GAMMA BANK—A RESEARCH CASE STUDY

Gamma Bank, owned by a Belgian bank, is a Fortune 100 financial institution with both retail and wholesale operations. In early 2001, the bank was facing a third year of declining profits and the possibility of red ink for the first time in its history. This downward trend had continued despite a recent large infusion of $800 million from its European owner. Prior to 2001 and the period of declining profits, Gamma had been led for ten years by a dynamic and dominating CEO and chairman, John Amato, who had greatly increased profits, sales, and market share during his tenure. When Amato retired in 1998, his second-in-command, Ralph Hines, succeeded him at age sixty-one. Hines had been a loyal but undistinguished subordinate to Amato. In contrast to the charismatic Amato, Hines was seen as a "quiet gentleman" who had emerged from years of obscurity while working in Gamma's finance department.

Shortly after becoming chairman and CEO, Hines divided the bank into two divisions, retail and wholesale. Hines chose Bill Sheldon, age fifty-one, to be president of Gamma and gave him responsibility for the wholesale group. In addition, Hines selected Harry Katz, age forty-two, to be vice chairman in charge of the retail division. Sheldon had arrived at Gamma three years before and was widely seen as the "cool intellectual" in the top management group; Katz, recruited from a competitor in 1998, was known for his "aggressive but warm personality." Hines assigned responsibility for daily operations to Sheldon and Katz, while devoting his attention to the board, the financial community, and the European investor.

In late 2000, Hines, at the urging of Harry Katz, decided to replace the retiring vice president of human resources with an outsider, Chris Miller, age fifty, who had been a personnel director at a Fortune 100 bank. Miller was given the title of executive vice president and was a member of the executive committee, which included Hines, Sheldon, Katz, and James Samuels, who resided in Brussels as vice chairman in charge of Gamma's International operations.

Miller spent his first three months interviewing executives and workers throughout Gamma. In his report of findings to the executive committee, he stated that "significant morale problems exist at all levels" and that "many people perceive a lack of strategic direction for the bank." He also noted, but did not report to the committee, that there seemed to be a "growing feeling that Gamma was being run like two separate companies." The executive committee directed Miller to look into the morale problem and develop a program to deal with it. He then began a search for an outside consultant to provide assistance. Gamma had a long history of using management consultants in its functional areas and in strategic planning.

Through various contacts and referrals, Chris Miller phoned Professor Rob Frank at a local university and asked Frank if he could stop by for a visit. Miller and Frank met to discuss the situation for about an hour, at which point Frank referred Miller to a faculty colleague, Barry Johnson, who was well known in the motivation and job design field. Frank did not feel sufficiently qualified himself to deal with the problems of low morale at Gamma.

Chris Miller, after meeting with Johnson, was sufficiently impressed to invite Johnson to make a presentation to Gamma's management council. The council consisted of fifteen members, including the executive committee members and their immediate subordinates. Miller asked Johnson to describe how a quality-of-working-life (QWL) program might be introduced in a selected part of Gamma's operations as an experiment to improve morale and performance.

Johnson, on returning from making his presentation to the council, told Rob Frank that he had never attended a meeting where, as he put it, "so much one-upmanship was going on among the participants." He said that the chairman, Ralph Hines, had remained quiet throughout the meeting and that Katz acted "less than enthusiastic," leaving before the meeting was over. Chris Miller later left a phone message for Johnson saying that Gamma had decided not to adopt a QWL program.

Two months later, Chris Miller phoned Frank again to arrange a second visit for the purpose of locating another consultant. On this occasion, Miller reported that "political differences" made it difficult for Gamma's senior management to agree to do a QWL project. As a result, Miller asked Frank if he could recommend another consultant who might work with Gamma in "charting a new strategic direction." Miller also told Frank that an academic consultant probably would not be effective because of "top management's skepticism toward professors."

As they talked, Miller described the political situation at Gamma as involving an underlying conflict between Chairman Hines, President Sheldon, and Vice Chairman Katz. He said that Sheldon and Katz did not respect Hines and that there was a lot of tension among the three. According to Miller, Hines believed that "competition between key managers is healthy for the profit center concept." Miller then confided to Frank that he had not told Hines that "Sheldon and Katz were not taking major decisions to Hines." Instead, as Miller explained to Frank, "Sheldon and Katz had formed a Thursday morning group"—composed of themselves, a couple of key subordinates, and Miller—to discuss important operating issues. According to Miller, "Sheldon and Katz each saw themselves as a logical successor to Hines." However, Miller pointed out to Frank that Sheldon and Katz were "not fighting publicly or privately with each other."

A few days later, Rob Frank called Chris Miller to recommend Strategic Management Associates (SMA), a major management consulting firm that had established a strong reputation in strategic planning projects, as well as an ability to bring consensus to a top management group. Miller indicated an interest, so Frank arranged for Miller to meet with two of SMA's "most experienced consultants," Bob Hagen and Rich Jones. Miller had warned Frank previously that any consultant who worked on the project would have to be acceptable to Sheldon and Katz.

Chris Miller, in an initial meeting with the two SMA consultants, described his perceptions of Gamma's competitive problems: "The bank is drifting in the marketplace." He also spent considerable time discussing the personalities of Sheldon and Katz. The two senior consultants listened intently and asked occasional questions, after which they described SMA's background and clientele, including how they would likely approach a study of Gamma's problems. Miller liked what he heard and decided to arrange for the consultants to meet with Sheldon and Katz.

The time of this second meeting was changed four times by either Sheldon or Katz, but finally after a month, a one-hour meeting was arranged. During this meeting, the SMA consultants did most of the talking in response to an initial question from Katz, who asked about their personal backgrounds and previous clientele. Sheldon and Katz reacted in a friendly manner, while both placed blame for Gamma's problems on "changes in the industry." At the end of the meeting, as they stood shaking hands, Katz invited SMA to submit a written proposal for a first stage of field research to "ascertain the nature of Gamma's strategic problem." Miller was delighted with the outcome.

A proposal was written and submitted by SMA, stating, "The purpose of the project is to determine the nature of the strategic problem facing Gamma through interviews with the top seventy officers and an examination of financial and marketing data." The proposed fee was $900,000, and the proposal concluded by stating, "If this first stage goes well, a second stage focused on implementation planning will be proposed."

Two months passed before Chris Miller called Bob Hagen to say that approval had been given for the project. He told Hagen, "I had an easy time getting agreement from the chairman, but it was difficult getting Sheldon and Katz together at the same time to sign off."

The first stage of the project was to be completed over a two-month period, yet it took almost four months to finish because of scheduling difficulties. During the project, the consultants had intended to meet informally with the Thursday morning group every two weeks to report on their progress, but these meetings were postponed three times at the last minute. When these meetings did occur, Sheldon and Katz were rarely present together. In making their reports, the SMA consultants gave a brief summary, usually confined to data-gathering steps that had taken place. Any substantive comments they made were limited to general observations, such as, "We're finding a lot of different points of view about what the strategy of Gamma is and should be." The Thursday morning group always listened with interest and encouraged the consultants to continue.

About halfway through the project, one of the senior consultants, Bob Hagen, happened to meet the chairman, Ralph Hines, at the local airport. Hines invited Hagen to ride into the city with him. During the trip, Hines asked Hagen about the project, and Hagen gave him an informal report, highlighting one finding that "a large shortfall seemed to exist between budgeted cost savings and the amount that several key executives believed can actually be saved." Hines expressed surprise but did not inquire further.

Shortly after that, Chris Miller called SMA to request that Bob Hagen be removed from the project because Sheldon and Katz had complained separately to him about Hagen's comments about the budget shortfall on the airport ride with Hines. Apparently the chairman had returned to his office from the airport ride and called in Sheldon and Katz separately, asking each to explain the budget discrepancy. Both denied that a shortfall existed. Miller told SMA that Sheldon and Katz still wanted to complete the consulting project because of its potential value, but that Hagen had to be removed from the project. A different interpretation of these events was later given by the remaining senior consultant, who said, "We had learned too much about Gamma.... Lower-level executives were too favorable toward the project for us to be fired ... so we replaced Bob Hagen, who had a lot of other work to do anyway."

The project continued as before, including sporadic meetings with the Thursday morning group. Sheldon usually attended, but Katz was seldom present. When the final report was ready, a presentation was made with slides to the Thursday morning group, which reacted favorably. The report called attention to a "lack of agreement on corporate strategy among Gamma's senior executives, as well as to a number of formal systems that seemed to be in conflict with each other, such as budgets with compensation." The same report was also given to Gamma's management council, including Ralph Hines who was in attendance. Again, the report was well received.

Shortly after, Chris Miller asked SMA to prepare a second proposal on "implementation planning." The proposal was immediately written and submitted, with estimated fees of $700,000, which were to cover a further investigation of the strategy and preparation of an action plan. Within two weeks, Chris Miller called SMA to say that the proposal had been approved.

During the second stage of implementation planning, the same scheduling problems continued with the Thursday morning group; only two meetings were held, with neither Katz nor Sheldon in attendance at the same time. Nevertheless, both Sheldon and Katz separately indicated in contacts with Miller that they were pleased with the project to date.

As the final report neared completion, a surprising and unexpected event occurred. The European majority shareholder suddenly decided to take charge of Gamma and sent its vice chairman, Henry Francis, to reside at Gamma's headquarters. It had acted, with the agreement of Gamma's board and Ralph Hines, because of their shared concern for Gamma's deteriorating profit position. Francis was appointed as vice chairman of Gamma, reporting directly to Hines. Francis planned to reside at Gamma headquarters until he completed a full assessment of Gamma's situation, after which he would submit recommendations to Gamma's board and its European shareholder.

Gamma's senior management was stunned by the move, as were SMA's consultants. Chris Miller informed SMA about the move and asked SMA to postpone its final report on implementation for a few weeks until he could become better acquainted with the new vice chairman. Four weeks later, Chris Miller asked SMA to make its report on implementation to Francis (the new vice chairman). SMA gave its final report orally with slides to Francis, Hines, and Chris, as well as Katz, who requested at the last minute to be allowed to sit in. The vice chairman listened thoughtfully, asked several questions, and took a few notes. The other parties remained silent. At the conclusion, Francis warmly thanked the consultants, saying that he would like to meet privately with them in a few weeks.

SMA heard nothing from Gamma until four weeks later, when an SMA consultant learned from an executive at Gamma that Katz was "rumored to be on his way out." One week later, the newspapers reported that both Katz and Sheldon had resigned. Three days later, the newspapers reported that a new president had been appointed from outside the bank to replace Sheldon, but Katz's position was not filled. The new president was placed in charge of the entire bank, reporting directly to chairman Hines. The vice chairman from the European shareholder, Henry Francis, announced that he was returning to his Brussels base.

Two months later, the SMA consultants, not having heard from Gamma, called Chris Miller, who said, "It is too early for SMA to make their report to the new president" and that "I will get back in touch with you as soon as it seems appropriate." Two months passed without a call from Miller. The consultants were puzzled; they had made over $1.6 million in fees, yet there had been no call.

# Appendix C

## PETROFUELS ENERGY– A RESEARCH CASE STUDY

Petrofuels Energy, with revenues exceeding $950 million, was the fifth largest marketer and distributor of fuels to consumers in the United States. Headquartered in Denver, it employed five thousand people and served over 300,000 domestic, industrial, agricultural, and airports nationwide through terminals and delivery trucks. These outlets were fed by pipelines, rail tank cars, and a fleet of trucks located strategically at rail and truck terminals.

Petrofuels was a major subsidiary of Global Services, a $3.5 billion diversified corporation recently taken private through a leveraged buyout (LBO). According to Hank Jones, chairman and CEO of Global Services, the corporation's previous stock price on the New York Stock Exchange was undervalued at nearly half its book value, and he became worried about a hostile takeover. In commenting on the implications of the LBO for both Global and Petrofuels, Jones made the following observation: "The LBO flipped Global from having $300 million in equity and $100 million in debt to just the reverse. It made us private and more in control, but the cost of the increased debt was $45 million each year in interest. I was unhappy with the performance of Petrofuels and its ability to contribute to paying off the debt so I brought in Wil Martin to be CEO of Petrofuels."

The decision to bring in Martin as CEO was a difficult one that Jones hoped would produce a turnaround in earnings at Petrofuels. Jones had hired Martin as a management consultant immediately after the LBO to assist him in developing a cost reduction program at three of Global's subsidiaries, one of which was

Petrofuels. At the same time, and unrelated to Martin's project, Jones terminated the CEO of Petrofuels and assigned one of his corporate vice presidents to serve as the interim president until a permanent CEO could be selected. With regard to his selection of Martin, Jones reflected: "I think everybody was shocked by my bringing in a consultant and putting him in a line role, but I think it's something that Wil wanted to do, and my feeling was that he had a lot of ability, so why not turn him loose at it."

Martin was a former air force pilot with a B.A. in English and an M.B.A. from the University of Southern California. His initial job was in real estate finance for a large bank, but he soon left that to join a management consulting firm in Chicago. Over the next few years, he moved to two other management consulting firms, where he quickly became a partner and senior officer, eventually heading the Chicago office of the second firm. In deciding to accept the job at Petrofuels, Martin said: "Even though I had some qualms about moving to Denver, I took it because I wanted a shot at managing a major company. Also, I respected Hank Jones, and I felt like I had some respect from him coming in the door. I didn't see the Petrofuels job as an end in itself. Once it was up and running, I could move on to something bigger. Hank gave me lots of incentive with an ownership interest."

## Introduction of Wil Martin

Martin became CEO of Petrofuels on his thirty-eighth birthday. He was introduced to the senior management group by the outgoing and interim CEO at a hastily called meeting. Martin was surprised to learn that the departing CEO had provided no advance notice of his arrival and appointment as CEO:

> We were about to go into the meeting together when I asked the former CEO if he had told them about my appointment, and he said no. So I suggested that maybe he ought to go in and have a few minutes alone with them so they could adjust to the news. He went in and, in essence, said, "I'm going off to work at Global

headquarters, and Wil Martin is going to be your new president, so I'll bring him in." And I went in. They were all sitting there looking stunned and demotivated as hell. Nobody had told them that any inside candidates were being considered.

During the meeting, Martin made a few brief comments about how he looked forward to working with the group. "It was very uncomfortable ... they just stared at me." Shortly after the meeting, the former CEO called Martin to tell him that he had planned to fire one of the senior executives (the person in charge of marketing) because he didn't want "to leave Martin with a cancer in the organization." Martin thanked him for his call.

Martin was so angry about the way the ex-CEO had treated senior executives that he decided not to heed the advice of the former CEO to fire one of them: "I didn't trust the judgment of the ex-CEO. I decided to keep all of the people, give them incentives, go through the annual planning process, and if it didn't work, then clean house."

Martin entered a functional organizational structure (see Figure C.1) where he found the senior group, as he put it, "in a low state of executive morale." Martin was the third Petrofuels CEO in two years and, according to one senior executive, "teamwork had all but disappeared, with everyone defending their own turf." During his first few days on the job, Martin observed that the senior executives tended to remain in their offices, and no one was speaking to him or to each other. "I felt like they all had their eyes on me, waiting for me, and even daring me to do something."

## The CEO's Initial Actions

Wil Martin quickly discovered that Petrofuels was 25 percent behind its annual profit plan, with only five months remaining in the fiscal year. As a result, he decided to begin a series of meetings with his executive committee to plan how they could achieve the annual profit goal. Martin's decision to hold these planning

**Figure C.1 Current Organization Structure at Petrofuels**

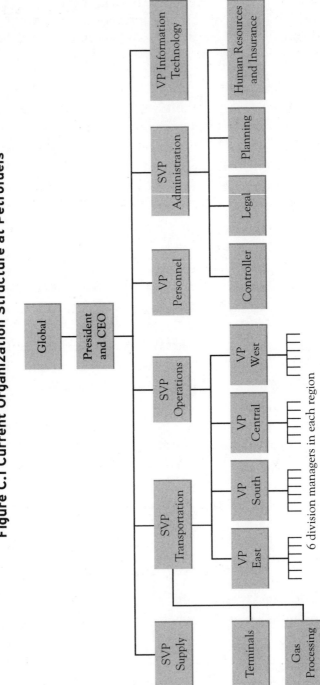

meetings was in contrast to the previous CEO's approach, which was to deal with people on a one-on-one basis. Martin described the subsequent meetings:

> It was an excellent forum that enabled me to ask questions, and that's why I enjoyed it. Very quickly, I learned a lot about the company. We came up with a laundry list of key issues, and airing them was a major improvement even though we couldn't solve all of them. What came out of all this was a commitment to achieve our profit goal for the year—and to hell with whether it was the right level, we would still try to achieve it.

Over the next few weeks, the planning meetings resulted in two major decisions and action steps taken by Wil Martin. One step was to arrange with Hank Jones for a revised incentive bonus for his key executives if they made the annual profit plan. The second was to raise prices immediately in order to increase revenues. The executive committee resisted Martin's pricing decision, but he stuck to it, saying, "Trust me."

At the end of five months, Petrofuels had exceeded its original profit plan by 10 percent, with half of its profits coming from the increase Martin had made and the remainder from increased unit sales. Martin called his executive committee together, congratulated them, and told them that they would all receive a substantial bonus. He also gave a gold clock to each member to remind them of "what they could do under time pressure." Martin was highly pleased with their accomplishments, and he felt that he could work with them in building on their backgrounds and prior experience: "From the start I liked what I saw. They were young, educated, and hadn't been in the company long enough to tell war stories. And then they really pitched in to pull it out."

Five months after Martin became CEO, he invited two of his former M.B.A. professors, Larry Greiner being one, to visit the company as a consultant. Greiner and Martin had remained close friends and colleagues since Martin's graduation ten years before. Over the years, Greiner had advised Martin on his career, which had been largely in management consulting, and on several occasions Martin had asked Greiner to work with him on consulting assignments.

On Greiner's initial visit to Petrofuels, Wil Martin asked him to interview his senior executives for issues that "they believe need to be addressed in the development of a long-term strategic plan," as well as "to get a reading on how I'm being perceived." They agreed that the interviewing effort should take place over about two days and that Greiner should give both an oral and a written report to Martin on completion. The consultant's fees were to be billed on a per diem basis. Greiner was assisted by Arvind Bhambri, an academic colleague of Greiner, who served as a researcher and consultant on the Petrofuels assignment.

The consultants, following their interviews with the executives, prepared a brief written report, which listed several major issues, including whether the company should diversify out of fuel to provide other services like tank and pipeline repairs, the adequacy of its existing organizational structure, and coordination problems arising from turf-protecting behavior among certain senior managers. Greiner told Martin that although the executives differed among themselves over proposed solutions to the strategic issues, they were "uniformly much happier under Martin's leadership." The consultant recommended that a retreat be held soon so that the top group could discuss strategic issues and come up with proposed solutions. Martin agreed because, he said, "we seemed to be making real progress as a team."

## First Workshop

Larry Greiner and Wil Martin planned the agenda for the first workshop and organized it around three broad topics: strategy for the company, organizational structure, and the top management team. The workshop was held at a "no-frills" hotel (requested by Martin), lasting from Friday noon to Sunday noon. Martin and his seven senior executives, all members of the Petrofuels executive committee, attended the workshop along with Greiner and Bhambri. Martin requested that Greiner serve as moderator so that he could participate with the others. "The group is looking to me too much," he said, "and I haven't all the answers. They have to become more active and vocal with their points of view."

In opening the workshop, Martin told the group, "I have no hidden agenda. I just want us to dive in and see where it takes us." Bhambri began with a short lecture summarizing lessons from the strategy literature and then used the SWOT framework in leading a discussion of Petrofuels's competitive situation. Several flip charts were filled when a heated interchange took place between Wil Martin and two members of the group:

Martin: Why do you guys see so many threats and so few opportunities?

March (vice president of transportation): Because the market for fuel is so mature and growth for fuel is limited.

Cook (vice president of supply): Besides, even if we could sell more fuel, we don't have enough money for investments because all our cash goes to Global to pay off the LBO debt.

Martin: I feel that we can take control of our own destiny, no matter what the others say. Let's don't blame others for why we can't take control.

The consultant then intervened to suggest that the group divide into two subgroups for the purpose of "identifying two to four alternative strategic directions for Petrofuels, along with the pros and cons for each alternative." Two hours later, they reported back, initiating a debate over two strategic alternatives: (1) diversification or (2) exclusive focus on fuel. Although Petrofuels had already diversified into a limited number of nonfuel businesses before Martin was appointed CEO, several members of the group were not as pleased with this direction, and the information technology member said, "There are still lots of opportunities in fuel if we make acquisitions and are more selective in our geographic markets." But another member, Jack Davis, the current head of marketing, argued strongly for diversification out of fuel. Martin remained quiet throughout this discussion, despite having participated actively in one of the subgroups.

The second day of the workshop again used subgroups to examine the issue of determining the best organizational structure for Petrofuels. The groups met after the consultant gave a short lecture on various structural alternatives, along with describing the conditions under which they might apply. One subgroup proposed a decentralized product structure divided between industrial and retail divisions, and the other advocated staying with the current functional organization structure.

The ensuing discussion became argumentative and wandering, with one member finally observing, "We can't solve this problem until we decide on our overall business strategy." Everyone seemed to agree, at which point Martin suggested that the group return to the strategy discussion. Bhambri then gave a brief lecture on designing a strategy statement. He told the group that the statement should "sum up the company's future competitive logic, be brief and clear, put into writing, and be made understandable to all employees." Two new subgroups were then assigned to draft suggested statements of strategic direction for Petrofuels.

At the end of the second day, each subgroup presented surprisingly similar strategy statements. Both subgroups seemed to agree that Petrofuels should "concentrate exclusively on the fuel industry," "become more marketing oriented," "make acquisitions," and "set high financial goals." Their discussions had determined that Petrofuels, despite being in a mature industry, could still "clean up," as they put it, because its major competitors were "badly managed" and there were many small "mom-and-pop" operations that might sell out. They then said they could charge more for providing better service and assurances of safety than their competitors could.

The remaining discussion centered on how high their financial goals should be; a central concern was how Petrofuels could still generate cash for Global while also making investments in acquisitions and additional marketing programs. A way out of this dilemma was found when one member proposed selling off the nonfuel assets, closing down low-profit fuel outlets, and cutting operating costs. When another member suggested that the company should try to "double profits in five years," Martin said, "I could be very excited by that goal, and I know I can sell it to Global."

The workshop ended on Sunday with Martin complimenting the group and leading them in a discussion about follow-up steps. It was agreed that each person should draft a separate strategy statement and give it to another member, Bill Hope, for final drafting of a single statement. Martin asked that the final draft be "subjected to some hard market and financial analysis" and that "it should be tried out in some group meetings with middle managers for their reactions." Martin then announced that the group would meet again in five weeks for a second workshop to "ratify a new strategy statement and resume discussion on organization structure."

## Second Workshop

The second workshop began with a presentation by Bill Hope of the final draft strategy statement. Everyone quickly indicated approval, with one member thumping his agreement on the table. For the rest of the morning, two subgroups met to evaluate the statement against a number of criteria provided by the consultants, including these questions: "Is it realistic in its assumptions about the marketplace and what we might be able to achieve?" "Is it sufficiently clear and easy to communicate?" "Do we find the statement exciting and challenging?" "Is it enduring but also selective enough to aid in screening major decisions?"

When the two groups returned, they reported that the draft statement met most of the criteria, but they also wanted it shortened and to include a more explicit focus on increased fuel marketing. Jim Dunn, head of supply, then drafted an abbreviated statement over lunch. When he read the following redrafted statement to the group in its afternoon session, spontaneous applause broke out:

> Petrofuels is a leading marketer and distributor of fuels to a broad range of customers at the retail and wholesale levels. We set aggressive financial goals and achieve growth through market development and acquisitions. Our people establish a competitive advantage in selected market segments through a unified effort that demands:
>
> • A strong marketing orientation
> • High standards of safety
> • Outstanding service "before our customers need us"

The remainder of the workshop proved far more difficult as the group turned to discuss the company's organizational structure. The consultant presented the two alternatives that had received the most attention at the first workshop: (1) a new product structure divided between wholesale and retail markets and (2) the existing functional structure. Again, the two subgroups were sent off separately to review the alternatives in terms of pros and cons. This time, however, each subgroup was asked by the consultant to determine which structure, or refinement thereof, would better implement the new strategy statement.

On returning from their subgroup meetings, both groups indicated a strong preference for the current functional structure, contending that the wholesale market did not show enough profit potential to warrant a separate product group. But here the agreement ended. One member argued for an entirely new marketing department that would develop new products and sales programs and transform the current marketing department into an operations group responsible for sales and distribution. But Jack Davis, the current head of marketing, retorted, "I can take care of all that in my department." When one member proposed the consolidation of all staff functions under a single senior vice president of administration, the directors of legal, human resources, and data processing all argued that they should continue to report directly to Martin. Time was running out when one member said, "Well, at least we know that we don't want a product structure, but will we ever agree on what we do want?"

The workshop ended with Martin expressing his personal commitment to the new strategy statement and then added, "We need to do some more thinking about our organization structure, so let's keep talking about it until our next workshop in one month."

## Third Workshop

Martin decided to become more directly involved in planning the agenda for the third workshop. He told the consultants: "We need to move these meetings off the discussion level and into action. I'm ready to move, and the group seems ready too. They seem to be waiting for me to make a decision, so I will do it. All our financial and marketing checks on the strategy statement make sense, and the middle managers like it. They say it isn't us now, so the question centers on implementation—especially, organization structure and who fills what jobs."

During a four-hour planning meeting prior to the third workshop, Martin and the consultants drew up a proposed organization structure (Figure C.2). Martin wanted to lead off the workshop with a presentation of the proposed structure, including a statement of key charters for each major function. He also wanted to hold an open discussion about who should fill what positions. The consultants agreed to design a format for handling this delicate discussion. Martin further decided to invite only the four senior vice presidents of the major functions to the workshop because "these guys are most crucial to making this happen, and I have to focus on their anxieties."

The third workshop began with Martin making a presentation of his recommended organizational structure, displayed on a flip

## Figure C.2 Proposed Organizational Structure for Petrofuels

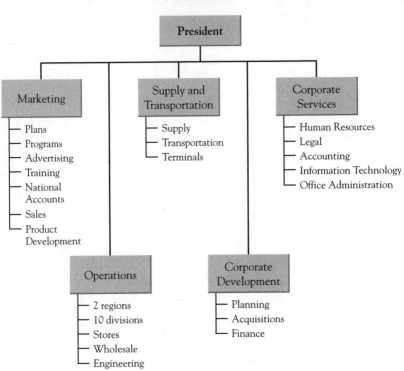

chart. It contained several changes from the current organization: adding a new marketing department, with the old one renamed "operations"; adding a corporate development group for acquisitions; combining the supply and transportation departments for better service to customers; and placing human resources, data processing, and legal all under a single senior vice president of corporate services. In addition, Martin explained to the group that he wanted to reduce the number of zone managers from four to two and regional managers from twenty-four to ten in operations (the old marketing department), so as to "tighten up management and put our best field managers against the marketplace." When he had finished his presentation on organization to the four senior vice presidents, he invited them to "criticize my proposal for how well it implements our new strategy. . . . Feel free to shoot holes in it," he said.

The group's discussion started slowly with mainly questions of clarification. The most silent member, Jack Davis, suddenly spoke up with a dissenting opinion: "I'm worried about the new marketing group being separated from my operations group." Martin responded sharply, "Jack, I want us to talk about these functions without putting ourselves in certain jobs."

Martin went on to explain that he felt marketing issues would not receive sufficient attention if left in operations and that he was trying to be consistent with the group's expressed desire to emphasize marketing in the new strategy statement. Other members seemed to agree with Martin's reasoning. Then one member suggested that national sales should be placed under the new marketing department, and Martin agreed. Another senior vice president felt that ten division managers were too few, so four more were added. After two hours of discussion and modifications, no one seemed to be raising further objections to the new structure, including Jack, who had confined his concerns to the new marketing department. Late in the day, one of the group said, "It looks good to me. Let's go ahead with it." The rest of the group vocally concurred, with Jack quietly nodding his head.

The next morning began with an active discussion to define key responsibilities for each top position in the new structure. When the group had finished drawing up these responsibilities, Martin said, "Now I would like to talk about who should fill each job, and I'd like to get your opinions and preferences." The consultant then asked the group to engage in an exercise where the participants were asked to put down on paper which jobs were their first and second choices, and who besides themselves, from inside or outside the group, would best fit each job. Much nervous laughter accompanied completion of the written assignment. When the final results were posted, the group was astonished to see exact agreement between their personal job preference and the nominations by their colleagues, with one notable exception:

the group preferred that Jack take the new marketing job, but he wanted to stay in his old job, now to be called operations. The marketing job was Jack's second choice.

Much of the subsequent discussion involved members of the group trying to persuade Jack to take the marketing job, but he strongly resisted. Finally, Martin stepped in: "Look, I feel very good about the way we have handled this. We seem to know where our basic talents match up. It's been a long day, so why don't we go off and relax a bit, and then we can return to our discussion after dinner."

Just as Martin was leaving the room, he quietly told the consultants "to order champagne and dinner for 7:00 . . . we are going to celebrate." Then he ran out the door after Jack, and they headed off for a walk together. Three hours later, the group returned for dinner, where Jack announced that he wanted to take the new marketing job. The group applauded, and Martin raised his glass to say: "I'm ready to go with all of you in new positions, so let's toast our goal of doubling over the next five years and all of us having a lot of fun doing it."

When the consultant later asked Martin what had happened with Jack, he explained:

> I told Jack that I really needed him in the marketing job because he was the best marketing person in the company. He still resisted. So I asked him what it would take to get him in the job, and to my surprise he said that he wanted responsibility for recruiting a bunch of young high-potential managers from his alma mater. And I said that was fine with me, at which point he jumped up and shook my hand. I was amazed, because I was ready to let him go.

The next morning they worked on action steps and finalizing the strategic statement. They listed each initiative on the board and suggested action steps to implement it. Everyone on the team had done their homework and brought lists themselves. The groups proposed several steps such as repainting the delivery trucks, requiring all drivers to appear in new uniforms, and training drivers how to treat customers in a friendly, service-oriented manner. Others not at the meeting had sent in their suggested action steps to Wil Martin. Everything went smoothly because there was a lot of consensus among them about action steps.

## Follow-Up and Results

The week following the third workshop was a busy one for the senior executives. Martin met separately with each of the three executives who were not invited to the workshop. One of them, the head of legal, had been nominated at the workshop and approved by Martin to be the new senior vice president of corporate services, which would encompass information technology, human resources, accounting, and legal. The legal executive was elated to hear about his promotion; the other two executives were disappointed yet supportive of the overall structural changes. Martin asked the new senior vice president of corporate services to meet immediately with the other two managers to discuss "how we can work together effectively as a team in the new organization."

Martin also asked the new executive committee, now consisting of five senior vice presidents instead of the earlier four senior vice presidents and three vice presidents, to meet in an all-day session. He asked each person to prepare in advance a new organization chart for each of their departments and to bring a list of nominations for persons in each job in their revised organizations. This meeting, attended by the consultant, saw the group review, modify, and approve various structural changes within each department. During the discussion about personnel appointments, two members argued over wanting to recruit the same manager, and Martin intervened: "Why don't you both talk to her and see which position she really wants to take?"

Two weeks later, a large celebration was held in the company's central warehouse with all field managers and corporate employees in attendance. A gigantic banner, "Double in Five Years," was displayed prominently, and a Dixieland band played. Martin gave a speech about the new strategy and the organization changes. Other senior executives stood nearby and spoke briefly with enthusiasm and support for the many changes. Employees in the audience seemed excited, and one manager asked Martin, "Will we have an opportunity to buy stock in the company?" Martin responded that it would be literally impossible under the LBO arrangements, but that "we will try to share the benefits with you."

During the following year, numerous changes occurred in Petrofuels, and its performance increased significantly. The first month saw thirty-nine executives change positions within the company, including all of the top executive team except for Wil Martin. Dramatic improvements in morale were cited by many employees in surveys. Several people reported numerous examples of senior and middle-level managers involving their subordinates more frequently in team decision making, and many employees were recognized for coming forward with new ideas and suggestions for additional changes.

The new head of marketing, Jack Davis, recruited five new young managers. The senior vice president of supply and transportation dominated the futures market on propane and became a supplier to other major propane users at a substantial profit. The asset base of the company changed dramatically as various nonfuel assets were sold off and five acquisitions were made of smaller fuel companies.

## Fourth Workshop

Martin called a fourth workshop for the executive team to "extend the change effort down to the lowest levels of the company." The consultant, Larry Greiner, moderated the meeting, although Martin and his team designed its format. During the meeting, the two remaining zone manager jobs in operations were eliminated and their job occupants transferred or retired, removing one entire level from the field hierarchy. Additional initiatives were launched leading to several programs with different senior executives taking responsibility for each new program. For example, a training program was created for sales managers, and a sales incentive program was introduced. A new profit-sharing plan was also created for all employees. Finally, all store managers were invited to bring their best salesperson with them to a two-day conference in Denver where Wil Martin discussed the company's strategic goals, followed by small group discussions and group reports on how to implement the strategic statement at the store level.

A manager two levels removed from the senior group commented later on the effects of the many changes in the company on him personally: "I was just about ready to leave when the lights came on. I got a new boss who finally listened to me. He was giving me a lot more work than I had before." Still another manager at the store level said: "Before Wil Martin, the guys at the head office rarely ever visited my store, and then it was to find something wrong. Now I feel like they are actually trying to help me. My sales have gone up a lot, and my paycheck is a lot fatter too."

## Results

At the end of one year, the company had greatly exceeded its profit plan, and its return on assets was up 40 percent. A sizable reward distribution was made to many employees from the profit-sharing plan. Special recognition was given to the senior vice president of corporate services, who came in $500,000 under budget. After two years, Wil Martin reported to Hank Jones that Petrofuels would double its profits in less than three years.

Over the next few years, continuous high performance took place. The top team continued to meet to look at their strategy and make revisions. They concluded that the competitive logic of market position and tiebreakers was sound and effective. Goals and initiatives were replaced with new ones. Acquisitions continued.

After five years, the company was sold as part of the LBO for a high return on the original investment, with an agreement that all employees could retain their jobs with the new owner for at least two years.

# Appendix D

## JOHNSON & JOHNSON STATEMENT OF STRATEGIC DIRECTION

*Source*: Aguilar, F. J., and Bhambri, A. "Johnson & Johnson (A)." Boston: Harvard Business School Case 9-384-053, Aug. 19, 1983.

We believe the consistency of our overall performance as a corporation is due to our unique form of decentralized management, our adherence to the ethical principles embodied in our Credo, and our emphasis on managing the business for the long term. There are certain basic principles that we are committed to in this regard:

- The responsibility for our success as a corporation rests in the hands of the presidents and managing directors of our companies. Each must assume leadership in every facet of the business, including the definition of strategic plans and providing for management succession.

- We will attempt to organize our businesses based on the clearly focused needs of the end users of our products and services. In many instances business units will be structured around the worldwide franchise philosophy. We will continue, however, to rely on "umbrella" companies to develop local markets for any of our franchises where this appears to be the best way to initiate cost effective, long-term growth.

- We will seek, where possible, to achieve or maintain a leadership position in our markets of interest. It is recognized that this can only be accomplished through maintaining, over the long term, end benefits superior to our competition. In this regard, we are committed to improving our internal research and development capability, and to utilizing external sources that provide access to new science and technology.

- We are dedicated to exceptionally high growth. To achieve this we must be well positioned in growth markets, and each management must be aggressively innovative and strive to grow faster than the markets in which it competes.

- Each management must know how to invest effectively in future earning power while recognizing that it is easier to reduce profits short term than to increase them long term. We further believe that growth should be financed primarily from earnings. This means our companies must generally make above average profits to support higher rates of growth.

- Acquisitions are viewed as an appropriate way to achieve the strategic goals of a given company or as a way for the corporation to expand the scope of its current business. Such acquisitions—of products, technologies, or businesses—will be evaluated for growth potential, fit with current or future businesses, management capacity, and economic feasibility. There are no other restrictions on the identification of acquisition candidates.

Corporate management is responsible for providing resources, guidance, leadership, and control of the various business entities within the framework of these principles. Management's most important responsibility is the one it shares with presidents and managing directors in attracting the kind of people who can manage our businesses in the future, providing them with the kind of environment that maximizes their potential and with a system that rewards them appropriately for their accomplishments.

# References

Abrahams, J. *101 Mission Statements from Top Companies*. Berkeley, Calif.: Ten Speed Press, 2007.

Amburgey, T., Kelly, D., and Barnett, W. "Resetting the Clock: The Dynamics of Organizational Failure." *Administrative Science Quarterly*, 1993, *38*, 51–73.

Andersen, M., and Poulfelt, F. *Discount Business Strategy: How the New Market Leaders Are Redefining Business Strategy*. Hoboken, N.J.: Wiley, 2006.

Andrews, K. *The Concept of Corporate Strategy*. Homewood, Ill.: Dow-Jones Irwin, 1971.

Ansoff, I. *Corporate Strategy*. New York: McGraw-Hill, 1965.

Argyris, C. *On Organizational Learning*. Oxford: Blackwell, 1999.

Barnard, C. *The Functions of the Executive*. Cambridge, Mass.: Harvard University Press, 1938.

Barney, J. "Firm Resources and Sustained Competitive Advantage." *Journal of Management*, 1991, *17*(1), 99–120.

Bartlett, C., and Ghoshal, S. *Managing Across Borders*. Boston: Harvard Business School Press, 1998.

Bartlett, C., and Wozny, M. "GE's Two-Decade Transformation: Jack Welch's Leadership." Boston: Harvard Business School Press, 2000.

Beer, M., and Eisenstat, R. "How to Have an Honest Conversation About Your Business Strategy." *Harvard Business Review*, Feb. 2004, pp. 82–89.

Beer, M., and Nohria, N. *Breaking the Code of Change: Resolving the Tension Between Theory E and O of Change*. Boston: Harvard Business School Press, 2000.

Black, J., and Gregersen, H. *Leading Strategic Change: Breaking Through the Brain Barrier*. Upper Saddle River, N.J.: Financial Times/Prentice Hall, 2002.

Block, P. *Flawless Consulting*. San Francisco: Jossey-Bass/Pfeiffer, 1999.

Boudreau, J., and Ramstad, P. *Beyond HR: The New Science of Human Capital*. Boston: Harvard Business School Press, 2007.

Bourgeois, L. J. III, and Singh, J. V. "On the Measurement of Organizational Slack." *Academy of Management Review*, 1983, *6*, 29–39.

Bower, J. *The CEO Within: Why Inside Outsiders Are the Key to Succession Planning*. Boston: Harvard Business School Press, 2007.

Bower, J., and Dial, J. "Jack Welch: General Electric's Revolutionary." Harvard Business School Case, No. 4, 1994.

Bower, J., and Gilbert, C. "How Managers' Everyday Decisions Create—or Destroy—Your Company's Strategy." *Harvard Business Review*, Feb. 2007, pp. 72–79.

Breene, P. F., Nunes, P., and Hill, W. "The Chief Strategy Officer." *Harvard Business Review*, Oct. 2007, pp. 84–94.

Bresser, R., Hitt, M., Nixon, R., and Heuskel, D. (eds.). *Winning Strategies in a Deconstructing World*. Hoboken, N.J.: Wiley, 2000.

Brown, S., and Eisenhardt, K. *Competing on the Edge: Strategy as Structured Chaos*. Boston: Harvard Business School Press, 1998.

Bryan, L., and Joyce, C. "Better Strategy Through Organizational Design." *McKinsey Quarterly*, May 2007, pp. 20–29.

Bunker, B., and Alban, B. *Large Group Interventions: Engaging the Whole System for Rapid Change*. San Francisco: Jossey-Bass, 1978.

Buono, A., and Bowditch, J. *The Human Side of Mergers and Acquisitions: Managing Collisions Between People, Cultures, and Organizations*. Frederick, Md.: Beard Books, 2003.

Bytheway, C. *Fast Creativity and Innovation: Rapidly Improving Processes, Product Development and Solving*. Fort Lauderdale, Fla.: J. Ross Publishing, 2007.

Cascio, W. *Managing Human Resources*. New York: McGraw-Hill/Irwin, 1986.

Colbert, A., Kirstof-Brown, A., Bradley, B., and Barrick, M. "CEO Transformational Leadership: The Role of Goal Importance Congruence in Top Management Teams." *Academy of Management Journal*, 2008, 51(1), 81–96.

Collins, J., & Porras, J. "Building Your Company's Vision." *Harvard Business Review*, 1996, 74(5), 65–77.

Cooperrider, D. L., Sorenson, P., Whitney, D., and Yeager, T. (eds.). *Appreciative Inquiry: Foundations in Positive Organization Development*. Chicago: Stipes Publishing, 2005.

Cope, R. *High Involvement Strategic Planning: When People and Their Ideas Really Matter*. Cambridge, Mass.: Basil-Blackwell, 1989.

Cruikshank, J. *Delicate Experiment: The Harvard Business School, 1908–1945*. Boston: Harvard University Press, 1987.

Davis, S. *Future Perfect*. Reading, Mass.: Addison-Wesley, 1996.

Davis, S., and Meyer, C. *Blur*. Reading, Mass.: Addison-Wesley, 1998.

Devane, T., and Holman, P. (eds.). *The Definitive Resource on Today's Best Methods for Engaging Whole Systems*. San Francisco: Berrett-Koehler, 2006.

Dye, R., and Sibony, O. "How to Improve Strategic Planning." *McKinsey Quarterly*, Aug. 2007, pp. 40–48.

Eisenhardt, K., Kahwajy, J., and Bourgeois, J. "How Management Teams Can Have a Good Fight." *Harvard Business Review*, July–Aug. 1997, pp. 77–85.

Eisenhardt, K., and Martin, J. "Dynamic Capabilities: What Are They?" *Strategic Management Journal*, 2000, *21*, 1105–1122.

Eisenhardt, K., and Sull, D. "Strategy as Simple Rules." *Harvard Business Review*, Jan.–Feb. 2008, pp. 106–116.

Finkelstein, S. "The Seven Habits of Spectacularly Unsuccessful Executives." *Ivey Business Journal*, Jan.–Feb. 2004, pp. 1–6.

Freedman, A., Zackrison, R., and Freedman, R. *Finding Your Way in the Consulting Jungle: A Guidebook for Organization Development Practitioners.* San Francisco: Jossey-Bass, 2001.

Gadiesh, O., and Gilbert, J. "Transforming Corner-Office Strategy into Front-line Action." *Harvard Business Review*, May 2001, pp. 72–79, 164.

Galbraith, J., Downey, D., and Kates, A. *Designing Dynamic Organizations: A Hands-on Guide for Leaders at All Levels.* New York: AMACOM, 2002.

Gerstner, L., Jr. *Who Says Elephants Can't Dance? Inside IBM's Historic Turnaround.* New York: HarperCollins, 2002.

Gladwell, M. *The Tipping Point: How Little Things Can Make a Big Difference.* Boston: Back Bay Books, 2002.

Gladwell, M. *Blink.* New York: Little, Brown, 2005.

Greiner, L. E., and Bhambri, A. "New CEO Intervention and Dynamics of Deliberate Strategic Change." *Strategic Management Journal*, Summer 1989, pp. 67–86.

Greiner, L., and Poulfelt, F. (eds.). *The Contemporary Consultant.* Cincinnati: Thomson Learning, 2005.

Greiner, L., and Schein, V. *Power and Organization Development.* Reading, Mass.: Addison-Wesley, 1989.

Hamel, G., and Prahalad, C. K. "Strategic Intent." *Harvard Business Review*, May–June 1989, pp. 63–76.

Heath C., and Heath, D. *Made to Stick: Why Some Ideas Survive and Others Die.* New York: Random House, 2007.

Henderson, B. *Henderson on Strategy.* New York: Signet, 1982.

Hickson, D., and others. *Top Decisions: Strategic Decisions in Organizations.* San Francisco: Jossey-Bass, 1986.

Hough, P. *Understanding Global Security.* London: Taylor and Francis, 2007.

Hsieh, T., and Yik, S. "Leadership as the Starting Point of Strategy." *McKinsey Quarterly*, Feb. 2005, pp. 66–73.

Janis, I. *Groupthink: Psychological Studies of Policy Decisions and Fiascoes*. Boston: Houghton Mifflin, 1982.

Jensen, M. "Self Interest, Altruism, Incentives, and Agency Theory." *Journal of Applied Corporate Finance*, Summer 1994, pp. 40–45.

Johnson, G., Langley, A., Melin, L., and Whittington, R. *Strategy as Practice: Research Directions and Resources*. Cambridge: Cambridge University Press, 2007.

Kahneman, D., and Tversky, A. "Prospect Theory: An Analysis of Decision Under Risk." *Econometrica*, 1979, 47, 263–292.

Kanter, R. "Transforming Giants." *Harvard Business Review*, Jan. 2008, pp. 43–93.

Kaplan, R., and Norton, D. *The Balanced Scorecard: Translating Strategy into Action*. Boston: Harvard Business School Press, 1996.

Kaplan, R., and Norton, D. "Mastering the Management System." *Harvard Business Review*, Jan. 2008, pp. 62–77.

Kim, W., and Mauborgne, R. *Blue Ocean Strategy: How to Create Uncontested Market Space and Make Competition Irrelevant*. Boston: Harvard Business School Press, 2005.

Kotter, J., and Cohen, D. (2002). *The Heart of Change*. Boston: Harvard Business School Press, 2002.

Lawler, E. E. III, and Worley, C. *Built to Change: How to Achieve Sustained Organizational Effectiveness*. Hoboken, N.J.: Wiley, 2006.

Lawler, E. E. III. *Organizing for High Performance: Employee Involvement, TQM, Re-Engineering, and Knowledge Management in the Fortune 1000*. San Francisco: Jossey-Bass, 2001.

Learned, E., Christensen, R., Andrews, K., and Guth, W. *Business Policy, Text and Cases*. Homewood Ill.: Irwin, 1969.

Lewis, H. *Choosing and Using Consultants and Advisors: A Best Practice Guide to Making the Right Decisions and Getting Good Value*. London: Kogan Page, 2004.

Lipton, M. *Guiding Growth*. Boston: Harvard Business School Press, 2003.

Lovallo, D., and Mendonca, L. "Strategy's Strategist: An Interview with Richard Rumelt." *McKinsey Quarterly*, 2007, no. 4, 56–67.

Markides, C. "A Dynamic View of Strategy." *Sloan Management Review*, 1999, 40, 1999, 55–63.

McKinsey. "Making the Board More Strategic — A McKinsey Global Survey." *McKinsey Quarterly*, Mar. 2008, pp. 1–10.

Mintzberg, H., Ahlstrand, B., and Lampel, J. (eds.). *Strategy Bites Back: It Is Far More and Less Than You Ever Imagined*. Upper Saddle River, N.J.: Prentice Hall, 2005.

Mintzberg, H., Lampel, J., and Ahlstrand, B. *Strategy Safari: A Guided Tour Through the Wilds of Strategic Management*. New York: Free Press, 1998.

Mintzberg, H., and Waters, J. "Of Strategies, Deliberate and Emergent." *Strategic Management Journal*, 1985, 6, 257–272.

Montgomery, C. "Putting Leadership Back into Strategy." *Harvard Business Review*, Jan. 2008, pp. 54–60.

Myers, D., and Bishop, G. "Discussion Effects on Racial Attitudes." *Science*, 1970, 169, 778–779.

Nadler, D., Behan, B., and Nadler, M. (eds.). *Building Better Boards: A Blueprint for Effective Governance*. San Francisco: Jossey-Bass, 2006.

Nadler, D., and Tushman, M. *Competing by Design: The Power of Organizational Architecture*. New York: Oxford University Press, 1997.

Obstfeld, M., and Taylor, A. *Global Capital Markets: Integration, Crisis and Growth*. Cambridge: Cambridge University Press, 2005.

O'Toole, J., and Lawler, E. III. *The New American Workplace*. New York: Palgrave Macmillan, 2007.

Owen, H. *Open Space Technology: A User's Guide*. (2nd ed.) San Francisco: Berrett-Koehler, 1997.

Pettigrew, A. *The Awakening Giant: Continuity and Change in Imperial Chemical Industries*. London: Blackwell, 1985.

Pfeffer, J. *Managing with Power: Politics and Influence in Organizations*. Boston: Harvard Business School Press, 1992.

Pfeffer, J. *The Human Equation: Building Profits by Putting People First*. Boston: Harvard Business School Press, 1998.

Phillips, J. *Investing in Your Company's Human Capital: Strategies to Avoid Spending Too Little—or Too Much*. New York: AMACOM, 2005.

Porter, M. *Competitive Strategy*. New York: Free Press, 1980.

Porter, M. *Competitive Advantage: Creating and Sustaining Superior Performance*. New York: Free Press, 1985.

Porter, M. "What Is Strategy?" *Harvard Business Review*, Nov.–Dec. 1996, pp. 60–78.

Rasiel, E., and Friga, P. *The McKinsey Mind: Understanding and Implementing the Problem-Solving Tools and Management Techniques of the World's Top Strategic Consulting Firm*. New York: McGraw-Hill, 2002.

Ready, A., and Conger, J. "Enabling Bold Visions." *MIT Sloan Management Review*, Winter 2008, pp. 70–76.

Robins, S. *Decide and Conquer: Making Winning Decisions and Taking Control of Your Life*. Upper Saddle River, N.J.: Prentice Hall, 2004.

Ronis, S. *Timelines into the Future: Strategic Visioning Methods for Government, Business, and Other Organizations*. Landham, Md.: Hamilton Books, 2007.

Rumelt, R. "How Much Does Industry Matter?" *Strategic Management Journal*, 1991, 12, 167–185.

Schein, E. *Process Consultation Revisited*. Reading, Mass.: Addison-Wesley, 1998.

Schein, E. *Organizational Culture and Leadership.* San Francisco: Jossey-Bass, 2004.

Schein, E., and Gallos, J. *Organization Development: A Jossey-Bass Reader.* San Francisco: Jossey-Bass, 2006.

Schwarz, R., Davidson, A., Carlson, P., and McKinney, S. *The Skilled Facilitator Fieldbook: Tips, Tools, and Tested Methods for Consultants, Facilitators, Managers, Trainers, and Coaches.* San Francisco: Jossey-Bass, 2005.

Scott, B. *Consulting on the Inside: An Internal Consultant's Guide to Living and Working Inside Organizations.* Alexandria, Va.: American Society for Training and Development, 2000.

Sheila, R. *Timelines into the Future: Strategic Visioning Methods for Government, Business and Other Organizations.* Landham, Md.: Hamilton Books, 2007.

Sheth, J. *The Self-Destructive Habits of Good Companies: And How to Break Them.* Philadelphia: Wharton School Publishing, 2007.

Slywotzky, A., Morrison, D., and Andelman, B. *The Profit Zone: How Strategic Business Design Will Lead You to Tomorrow's Profits.* New York: Times Business, 1997.

Snyder, W., and Cummings, T. "Organizational Learning Disorders." *Human Relations*, 1998, 51, 873–895.

Spencer Stuart study. 2007.

St.-Amour, D. "CEO Turnover and Job Security." New York: Drake Beam Morin, Sept. 2002.

Steiner, G. *Strategic Planning: What Every Manager Must Know.* New York: Free Press, 1979.

Stern, C., and Deimler, M. *The Boston Consulting Group on Strategy: Classic Concepts and New Perspectives.* Hoboken, N.J.: Wiley, 2006.

Swasy, A. *Changing Focus: Kodak and the Battle to Save a Great American Company.* New York: Random House, 1997.

Tufano, P. "How Financial Engineering Can Advance Corporate Strategy." *Harvard Business Review*, Jan.–Feb. 1996, pp. 135–146.

Ulrich, D., and Lake, D. *Organizational Capability: Competing from the Inside Out.* Hoboken, N.J.: Wiley, 1990.

Vancil, R. *Long Range Planning.* London: Pergamon Press, 1977.

Van de Ven, A. "Suggestions for Studying Strategy Process: A Research Note." *Strategic Management Journal*, 1992, 13, 169–188.

Voss, G. B., Sirdeshmukh, D., and Voss, Z. G. "The Effects of Slack Resources and Environmental Threat on Product Exploration and Exploitation." *Academy of Management Journal*, 2008, 51, 147–164.

Waltzer, N. (ed.). *Community Strategic Visioning Programs.* Westport, Conn.: Praeger, 1996.

Warren, K. *Strategic Management Dynamics.* Hoboken, N.J.: Wiley, 2007.

Weick, K. *Sensemaking in Organizations.* Thousand Oaks, Calif.: Sage, 1995.

Weisbord, M., and Janoff, S. *Future Search.* San Francisco: Berrett-Koehler, 1995.

Welch, J., and Byrne, J. *Straight from the Gut.* New York: Warner Books, 2001.

Wernerfelt, B. "A Resource-Based View of the Firm." *Strategic Management Journal,* Oct. 1984, pp. 171–180.

Williamson, O. "Strategizing, Economizing, and Economic Organization." *Strategic Management Journal,* 1991, *12,* 75–94.

Zook, C., and Allen, J. *Profit from the Core: Growth Strategy in an Era of Turbulence.* Boston: Harvard Business School Press, 2001.

# Index